Portraits
and recipes from
Tuscany

Beaneaters &bread soup

LORI DE MORI & JASON LOWE

To our parents:

Dinah, Jerry, Jilly, Millie, Rufus and Tony

with love and gratitude

INTRODUCTION 6

Introduction

It would be tempting to romanticise the postcard perfect version of Tuscany: olive groves, vineyards and woodlands spread out like a patchwork over a sea of rolling hills; stone farmhouses shimmering in the Mediterranean sunshine – were it not for the fact that Tuscans refuse to romanticise themselves. They still remember a time, not so long ago, when the day's main meal was nothing more than *pane e companatico* – bread and 'something to go with the bread.'

The quintessential 'something' was *fagioli* (beans) – *la carne dei poveri* (the poor man's meat) – usually dried white cannellini cooked overnight in an old wine flask nestled among the dying embers in the kitchen fireplace. The humble white bean – boiled with a sprig of sage, a clove of garlic and a few peppercorns, then scattered into soups, ladled on to toasted bread and doused with olive oil, or simmered with crushed tomatoes – was such a fixture in the Tuscan kitchen that *toscani* were nicknamed *mangiafagioli* by their fellow Italians. 'Beaneaters'.

The bread half of the *pane e companatico* equation was, and remains, a curious thing. The heavy golden loaves with their thick crusts and dense, chewy crumbs have everything you'd expect from a naturally leavened, hearth-baked bread. Everything but salt. The story goes that when Italy was still an unruly collection of city states, Pisa's neighbours responded to the maritime republic's imposition of a salt tax by baking their daily bread without it. *Pane sciocco* ('insipid' bread) balanced the earthy flavours of the Tuscan table so well that the habit of saltlessness evolved into an enduring tradition.

Of course, sometimes the 'something that went with the bread' was more bread. The laws of frugality in those lean days meant that nothing from the kitchen could ever be wasted or thrown away. And so, scraps of dry, stale bread would be revived from their petrified state into a soup or a salad of sorts. Tuscan standards like *ribollita* ('re-boiled' bread, cabbage and bean soup), *panzanella* (bread salad), and *pappa al pomodoro* (bread and tomato soup) owe their existence to two of the defining features of unsalted Tuscan bread: it can go hard without turning mouldy, and absorb liquid without becoming gluey. They owe their abiding popularity to the fact that they are far more delicious than they sound on the page.

The truly remarkable thing about the Tuscan kitchen of those times is that however unrelenting the need for parsimony, it was never greater than the twin beliefs that there should be flavour – even, or perhaps especially, where there was not abundance – and that creativity and resourcefulness would do more to satisfy the family's appetite than the grim-faced determination simply to provide sustenance.

The end of World War II brought unthinkable prosperity to Italy. *La campagna toscana* was virtually abandoned as farmers poured into the cities looking for jobs. The kind of cooking that wasted nothing, chose *nostrale* (local) over exotic and stayed faithful to the seasons was no longer a necessity. It was a matter of common sense. And so Tuscans still eat their beans. Not because they have to, but because there is no better vehicle for their beloved *olio di oliva*; because *fagioli* are, after all, delicious; and finally, because there's nothing wrong with eating beans – or for that matter, being called a Beaneater.

Beaneaters & Bread Soup tells two stories: the first, of a kind of cooking that is at once generous, frugal and inextricably tied to the land from which it comes; the second, of culinary artisans whose lives and work are held in much the same spirit.

The latter are Tuscans by choice or by birth – among them is a beekeeper, a knifemaker, a countess, a shepherd, a fisherman, a potter, and an assortment of farmers, winemakers, cooks and craftsmen whose work relates to the culinary arts. Collectively they inhabit the width and breadth of the Tuscan landscape, each carrying out his labours in due season: mushroom hunting when the weather is warm and damp; olive picking in autumn; lambing in spring. The potter's medium is earth and fire; the beekeeper's laboratory a wildflower strewn meadow. One cook works out of a monastery kitchen, another ladles tripe from the back of a three-wheeled scooter.

Beaneaters & Bread Soup was inspired by the quality of attention and care they bring to their labours, and the kind of wholeness to their efforts that blurs the line between work and life. As individuals they are unique in temperament, personality and the bare specifics of their lives. On an elemental level they are as alike as they are different, and share some essential qualities:

A kind of personal integrity that can be confused with eccentricity: 'however strange it may seem to you, this is the way I do things'.

Pride without arrogance: a sincere belief in the excellence of their work.

Humility and steadfastness: the ability to light the wood stove, milk the ewes, coax the bees out of their hives – quietly, without pretence – day after day, year after year.

The belief that their work is not a means to something else, but one of the ways to give meaning to their lives.

Genius: the brilliance that comes to those driven by their personal vision rather than by a desire for success, money or fame.

Generosity: they have no secrets. If you appreciate what they do, they'll tell you everything they know… and usually set a place for you at their table.

* * *

Gianluca Paoli

Cook/Proprietor: Coco Lezzone

6:00am inside a tiny kitchen on the corner of Via del Parioncino and Via del Purgatorio (Purgatory Street) in Florence's *Centro Storico* (historic centre) and Gianluca Paoli is already at work, feeding armfuls of oak kindling to an ancient cast-iron stove. He is, in fact, the only one at work – the rest of his crew won't begin to arrive until the civilised hour of 9:00am.

It doesn't seem to matter that Paoli is the owner of the celebrated *trattoria* Coco Lezzone and, as such, presumably able to delegate the awakening of a 200 year-old stove to someone else. Or that he has a beautiful wife and two *bambini* who might prefer he be home when they wake up in the morning. Firing up the stove is a task he is unwilling to hand over. '*Arista* (roast pork loin) is our *piatto forte*,' he says with a quiet earnestness that comes across as equal parts humility and pride. 'It needs to brown first thing in the morning when the cooker's really hot, then roast slowly so that it's ready by lunchtime.'

I'd eaten a dozen meals at Coco Lezzone before I realised Paoli was largely responsible for cooking them. It's hard to tell. He never toots his own horn and, for all his dawn antics in the kitchen, by mealtime he's in the dining room greeting customers. He's the antithesis of a celebrity chef… and a good thing too. Most of the Florentines who've tried to don that mantle are so arrogant it's hard to swallow their food, however delicious. His unobtrusiveness seems volitional rather than accidental, a tacit statement that this place is about the food, not about him.

Paoli describes himself as a *cuoco* (cook), not a chef. 'The men in my family all cook, and the women don't. Even at home. My mom can hardly boil an egg – neither can my wife. I learned to cook from my dad who was a builder by trade but brilliant in the kitchen. Even before he owned the *trattoria*, he loved to invite friends over for Sunday lunch. We'd have as many as 20 people squeezed around our table. When my mom started to panic he'd just take over and do everything.'

Gianluca was 9 years old when his father Gianfranco bought the *trattoria* – already named Coco Lezzone – from a friend in 1970. 'Some kind of food and wine has been served on the premises for the past 300 years,' he explains. 'In the 1800's it was a *mescita di vino*, selling unbottled wine and a few things to eat. They called it *la Vespa* (the Wasp) on account of the swarms of wasps constantly buzzing around the *mescita*,

the meat hung out in the street to age. Over the years the place has evolved into a full-fledged *trattoria*.'

Satisfied by the hiss and crackle of the stove's fire, Gianluca walks across the street to the restaurant's larder and pulls a whole pork loin from the fridge. First he 'drugs' the meat, using the end of a long-handled wooden spoon to push a mixture of chopped rosemary, sage, garlic, salt and pepper through the soft centre of the loin. Next he ties the *arista* – bones and all – with kitchen twine, scatters the fatty side with salt and peppercorns, douses the whole thing with olive oil and slides it into the oven. Then he heads down the street to the bar for an espresso.

Coco Lezzone's weekly menu is posted by the front door and looks like it was typed on an old Olivetti whose ribbon needs changing. It is spring, and under the heading *contorni* (side dishes) there are peas. That a dish of said *piselli* cooked with little chunks of *prosciutto crudo dolce* costs more than the beef stew is a good sign – it means the peas are fresh and hand shucked. Anyone who has ever spent an hour reducing a heap of bright green pods to a small bowl of *piselli* will appreciate the effort that goes into shucking peas for an entire restaurant.

The rest of the menu includes most of the dishes one would expect to find at a Florentine *trattoria* – things like *pappa al pomodoro* (tomato and bread soup), *trippa alla fiorentina* (tripe cooked with tomatoes) and the pantagruelian *bistecca alla fiorentina* – the city's most notable exception to the unspoken rule that all things should be eaten in moderation.

On the upper left hand side of the menu – under the heading 'IMPORTANTE' – the following caveats appear (in both Italian and English): 'The trill of mobile phones disturbs the *ribollita*'s cooking. This traditional Florentine establishment has always followed its own rules – we don't serve coffee and we accept traveller's cheques and any foreign currency, but not credit cards.' This intrigues. Not only is Florence a city that abounds with *trattorie* – most of them offering only the slightest variations on a well-worn theme, but the city doesn't feel like a place that would permit a restaurateur to make his own rules. Florentines are the sort of folk who tuck a bottle of *olio di oliva extra-vergine* in their hand luggage when they travel, and look for well-loved familiar flavours when they stay home. 'Florentines are the hardest customers. They expect to eat well and pay little. So I want everything we serve to be extraordinary. Traditional, but extraordinary.'

This isn't just chat. Take, for example, those little platters of prosciutto (more or less salty), salame of various persuasions, and other and sundry cured pork bits that begin a typical Florentine meal. Rare is the *trattoria* that cures its own meats. A local *contadino* raises a pair of hogs for Paoli every year from which he makes *sbriciolona* (a soft, crumbly salami flavoured with fennel seed) and a peppery *salame toscano* dotted with chunks of creamy pork fat. On the premise that it is better to make a few exceptional things than many ordinary ones, Paoli doesn't make prosciutto, but uses the hams in the salami.

Coco Lezzone's *bistecca* is legendary. Its cooking monopolises the wood stove, hence the requirement that it be ordered in advance. 'No one makes a steak like ours,'

says Paoli. In Italian this sounds something of a poetic statement of fact: '*La bistecca come si mangia qui non si mangia da nessuna parte*.' The stove makes all the difference. 'The trouble with cooking meat over wood is that the fat drips on to the embers, which flame up and ignite the meat. You end up with a smoky, bitter aftertaste we call *moccolaio*. Our old stove has such a strong draw that this just doesn't happen.'

By mid-morning the *trattoria* hums with life. Paoli's mother Grazia has arrived – petite, preternaturally cheerful, and bearing a bowl of apricots picked from a tree in her garden. Her husband smiles down at her from a black and white photograph on the wall. He cooked at the *trattoria* until his death a few years ago. Paoli's wife Cinzia arrives on a bicycle bearing their 2 year-old son Cosimo and a basket of bright yellow flowers which she begins to arrange into little posies for the tables.

Coco Lezzone has a homely beauty that pleases the senses without assaulting them. Two tiny rooms at the front are covered with thick, white tiles and yellowing photographs of illustrious guests – Luciano Pavarotti and Prince Charles among them. An airy room at the back has long, family-style tables whose red checked tablecloths are covered with small, crisp white ones. The walls are painted a deep, sombre ochre, which looks evocative in Tuscany and would look drab anywhere else. A chunky wooden cabinet holds rows of cutlery, stacks of neatly folded napkins and delicate, stemless wineglasses. Morning light streams through the windows. Ceiling fans whirr overhead. The place has the unpretentious appeal of certain sturdy, wide-hipped women – the sort who wear sensible shoes and whose gentle, open faces make you want to lay your head in their laps like a child. Utility and sensibility are on common ground here, and the effect is undeniably lovely.

While *nonna, mamma e babbo* are absorbed in their respective tasks, Cosimo toddles from room to room, all curly blond locks, chubby legs, blue leather shoes and curiosity. He drags a wooden chair to the pass-through window that looks into the kitchen, climbs on and watches his father at work. Paoli is a big man and the narrow galley kitchen looks impossibly small by comparison. '*Caldo* (hot), *brucia* (burn), *freddo* (cold),' Cosimo announces from his perch. I can't help wondering what he will be doing in 20 years time.

At 12:45pm the first customers start trickling in – local businessmen who tuck the white cloth napkins into their collars; gastronomically minded tourists looking for a quintessentially Florentine meal at one of the city's most famous *trattorie*; and habitués like local artist Alfio Rapisardi who salute each other by name and speak with the aspirated 'h' that identifies the Florentine accent (so that Coca-Cola sounds like 'ho-ha ho-la').

'People don't like the word *immobilità* (immobility) these days,' says Paoli surveying the bustling dining room. 'But it is the word that I think best describes this place. I am trying to safeguard the flavours and culinary traditions of a Florence that existed 100 years ago. The payoff for me is when someone says, 'this tastes just like the *pappa al pomodoro* my *nonna* used to make 50 years ago.' There's no better compliment.'

ARISTA DI MAIALE
ROAST PORK LOIN

SERVES 8

12 garlic cloves, finely chopped
4 tender rosemary sprigs (leaves only), chopped
handful of sage leaves, chopped
sea salt and freshly ground black pepper
2.5kg pork loin with bone
60ml olive oil

Preheat the oven to 250°C/Gas 10 (or its highest setting if your oven doesn't quite reach this temperature).

Combine the garlic and herbs in a bowl and season generously with salt and pepper. Push the handle of a long wooden spoon through the soft centre of the loin, boring a 2–3cm hole from one end of the roast to the other. Stuff the hole with the garlic and herb mixture.

Lay the meat, bone side down, in a roasting pan and rub with olive oil, then season with salt and pepper. Roast the pork in the oven for 30 minutes, then reduce the heat to 180°C/Gas 4 and cook until a long-tined fork inserted into the meat produces no liquid, about 1 hour. Lift on to a board, carve into thick slices and serve.

PAPPA AL POMODORO
TOMATO & BREAD SOUP

SERVES 6–8

250ml olive oil

3 garlic cloves, crushed

3 leeks, finely chopped

1 litre meat stock (made with beef and chicken)

2 litres puréed canned Italian tomatoes

500g day-old country bread (preferably unsalted), thickly sliced

generous handful of basil leaves, torn

sea salt and freshly ground black pepper

extra-virgin olive oil to drizzle

Warm the olive oil and garlic in a medium cooking pot. When the garlic has coloured slightly, add the leeks. Sauté over a low heat for 20 minutes, adding water as necessary to keep the vegetables from turning brown. Stir in the stock and puréed tomatoes and bring to the boil, then reduce the heat and simmer gently for 30 minutes.

Turn off the heat and add the bread, pushing it into the liquid with a wooden spoon. Stir in the torn basil leaves and season to taste with salt and pepper. Leave to rest for 30 minutes.

Now whisk the soup energetically until it has a porridge-like consistency. Taste and adjust the seasoning. Ladle into bowls, drizzle with extra-virgin olive oil and serve.

PISELLI SGRANATI
PEAS WITH PROSCIUTTO

SERVES 4

2kg young, fresh young peas in their pods
1 yellow onion, chopped
100ml extra-virgin olive oil
75g Italian prosciutto, diced
sea salt and freshly ground black pepper

Pod the peas and set them aside in a bowl. Put the onion and olive oil in a medium heavy-based saucepan over a low heat and sweat the onion, stirring frequently, until it is soft and translucent, but not browned, about 10 minutes.

Add the peas and prosciutto, stir well and pour in just enough water to cover. Cook, covered, for 10–20 minutes depending on the size of the peas, until they are soft but not mushy. Season with salt and pepper halfway through the cooking time.

TIRAMISÙ
TIRAMISU

SERVES 8

4 very fresh organic large eggs, separated
150g caster sugar
500g mascarpone cheese
250ml freshly brewed espresso coffee, cooled
24 sponge fingers
3 tablespoons cocoa powder
3 tablespoons dark chocolate shavings

Whisk the egg whites in a clean, dry bowl using a balloon whisk until stiff white peaks form.

In a separate bowl, beat the egg yolks and sugar together until the mixture thickens and turns pale yellow. Slowly incorporate the mascarpone and continue beating until the mixture is smooth and creamy. Use a large, metal spoon to gently fold in the egg whites, then set the bowl aside.

Pour the espresso into a shallow bowl. One at a time, dip each sponge finger into the coffee for a couple of seconds so it is moist but not saturated and place in a medium rectangular dish. Repeat with as many sponge fingers as it takes to cover the bottom of the dish, forming an even layer. Spoon half the mascarpone mixture over the top, then add a second layer of sponge fingers. Cover with the remaining mascarpone mixture and dust with cocoa powder and chocolate shavings.

Refrigerate until well chilled before serving.

Roberto Ballini

Beekeeper

Roberto Ballini wasn't always a beekeeper on the island of Elba. In his youth he was a professional cyclist, and even now in his 60's he has the sinewy body and bearing of an athlete. 'We ate honey for energy when we raced,' he explains, holding a small glass jar under a vat of rosemary honey and opening the spigot. 'Some people used sugar, but it's not as good. Honey is a pure, natural food… exactly the opposite of refined sugar. *Il miele è genuino*.'

The Italian word for honey – *miele* (pronounced 'mi-elle-ay') – is not so much onomatopoeic as it is sweet, fluid and a bit sticky in the mouth, just like the thing it represents. *Genuino* is another story altogether. The translation 'genuine' doesn't do justice to a word that when used in Tuscany evokes notions of purity, simplicity, wholesomeness and authenticity. Wine made the old way (i.e. not aged in wood, not made from foreign grapes) is *genuino*; so is honey from bees that sip from the sweet hearts of wildflowers.

Ballini is a portrait of *genuinità* himself. His arms are bare and tanned, and he carries a feather and a porcupine quill (both tools of his queen breeding trade) in the back pocket of his jeans. For the moment he's not dressed in a beekeeper's suit, or even wearing a hat. I wonder if he shares the view I've heard somewhere that bee stings are actually good for you. '*Ma*,' he answers, with raised eyebrows and the monosyllabic Italian expression of scepticism. 'I've been stung a thousand times and I ache all over.'

Beekeeping is common enough throughout Italy, but the island of Elba is famously rich in wildflowers. In spring, its hills and headlands are blanketed in rosemary, milk thistle, lavender, fennel, garlic, borage, heather, hawthorn, eucalyptus, myrtle, mallow and a thousand other wild and flowering things. Ballini believes there is no better place for keeping honey bees – or for breeding queens.

We walk around Roberto Ballini's apiary on the northeast end of the island in the hills above the village of Cavo. The sea sparkles clear and blue in the distance as if it's freshly awakened from a long winter's rest. Seagulls glide in the brightening sky and the air is sweet with the salt-tinged, cinnamony scent of the *macchia mediterranea*, the jumble of flowering scrub and trees that blanket the Mediterranean coastline. Wooden beehives on squat pedestals nestle among fruit trees, evergreen oaks and wildflowers, like a neighbourhood of ramshackle dollhouses.

You can hear the steady drone of the bees before you actually see them burrowing their heads into the flowers, far more interested in gathering sweetness than in causing us any harm. 'They love *cisto*,' says Ballini, pointing to a rock rose whose papery pink petals encircle sunny yellow centres. 'They go for the pollen, not the nectar,' he explains. Bees make honey from nectar, but they need pollen as a protein source. 'Some people keep bees just to help pollinate their crops,' he adds, stirring up memories of elementary school science class – pistils, stamens, ecosystems and the interdependence of all things. 'Sometimes the bees fall asleep with their heads in the flowers – it's as if they're drunk.' He points to the woolly yellow body of a bee sprawled over a *cisto* like a contented newborn asleep at the breast.

Ballini combines the meticulousness of a scientist, the observational powers of a naturalist and the bright-eyed curiosity of a child. 'It's not enough that a hive produces good honey: the bees need to be docile, adaptable to climactic changes, resistant to disease and able to take good care of the hive.' Every year he discovers something new about bees – things he's never come across in scientific journals. 'Last year I saw a bee scratching its back,' he exclaimed. 'It was like a little contortionist! I'd never seen a bee do that before. The implications are tremendous.' Honey bees, he tells me, suffer from mites. '*Poverini*, it's like they're flying around with turtles on their backs.' He reckons that bees could flick off the mites if their little legs were agile enough to reach around to their backs.

Ballini's even more excited about his latest discovery. We walk over to one of the hives. '*Vedi*, a little imagination can bring you to a reality you wouldn't otherwise discover,' he says, pulling out a wooden tray whose perfectly hexagonal latticework of honeycomb is covered with bees. 'Now watch this. Don't be alarmed.' He sucks in his breath, holds it for an instant, then barks out a high pitched: 'Aieee!' The bees freeze – every one of them, like a herd of deer caught in the headlights. They remain immobile for a split second, then it's back to work as usual. 'I have no idea why they do this, but I'm sure there's a reason. My kids think I'm completely mad.'

Ballini only started raising queens 15 years ago, but it seems to be the thing he's most passionate about. He pulls on his beekeeping gear – not so much the spacesuit of my imaginings as what looks like a yellow rain jacket with a mesh-fronted hood – and warns us to keep our distance. He lights a piece of cardboard, stuffs it into a small tin bellows and pumps a bit of smoke into one of the boxes. Then he carefully lifts out a wooden frame, upon which is not the usual configuration of comb, honey and bees, but two rows of queen bee larva at various stages of development.

He beckons us over and begins dusting off the peanut shaped cells with a feather. He uses the porcupine quill to do what he calls a *traslavo*. I'm not entirely sure what this is and my dictionary doesn't define it, but he does it the same way he does everything else – with laser bright attention. 'Only lost one,' he says, sliding the frame back into the box. '*Ho lavorato bene.*' He's not self-congratulatory – just pleased with the results of a job well done.

This week he's sending five queens to France. They are packed for shipping in separate little boxes, each accompanied by a retinue of worker bees. 'I've read a lot of books about beekeeping, but most of what I've learned has been from just watching the bees. It's true what they say you know – *dove mette la mano, l'uomo fa sempre danno.*' Man damages everything he touches. 'The bees know what they're doing; I just try not to interfere too much.'

Ballini Honeys

Ballini's honeys might come as a surprise to those who've never ventured beyond the wan, thin stuff found in little packets at second-rate hotels or inside plastic squeeze bottles shaped like bears.

Honey is made, after all, from the sweet nectar of flowers – collected by field bees who return to their hives and regurgitate their cache into the mouths of young worker bees, who in turn deposit the nectar into the hive's waxy hexagonal cells and perform whatever other alchemy necessary to complete the transformation into honey.

Nectar isn't a generic substance – just as lavender is not rosemary is not eucalyptus, neither are their nectars. Each has its own scent, flavour and consistency. Each will make its own honey. And though the blossoms of some flowering things smell like honey, strangely it isn't the other way around: pale, delicate rosemary honey isn't at all reminiscent of the herb itself.

Ballini uses honey wherever most people would use sugar. He doesn't cook with it because he doesn't cook – but he approves of the latest trend among Tuscan restaurateurs to pair a wedge of aged local sheep's cheese with a rich, strong honey like *castagno* (chestnut).

*MILLEFIORI/*WILDFLOWER He means it – a thousand flowers. The flavour differs slightly every season. Perfectly all-purpose honey.

*ROSMARINO/*ROSEMARY Ballini's favourite – Elba's wild rosemary is what got him started making honey in the first place. Clear, pale, sweet and delicately flavoured.

*CASTAGNO/*CHESTNUT Honey lover's honey – too sharply flavoured for the faint-hearted. Deep brown, liquid, smooth and caramelly.

*ERICA/*HEATHER An amber, crystallised honey, derived not from moor heather but from spring flowering Mediterranean *arboreous Erica*.

*CORBEZZOLO/*ARBUTUS Cloudy, pale grey-green, buttery honey with the consistency of toffee and a strong, bitter aftertaste. Rare.

*LAVANDA/*LAVENDER Sweet scented, pale, golden and delicate.

*EUCALIPTO/*EUCALYPTUS Dense, amber-coloured honey, with hints of balsam and mineral salts.

*MELATA/*TREE SAP HONEY Made from the sweet sap of certain trees rather than from nectar. Dark molasses brown, high in minerals and slightly malty.

*CARDO/*THISTLE A rare, reddish-amber coloured crystallised honey, which has an intense spicy scent.

*ELICRISO/*STRAWFLOWER Ballini's most controversial honey, if there can be such a thing. The silvery leafed plant smells like the distilled essence of the *macchia mediterranea*. 'We made the honey, then scientists told us bees couldn't make honey from *elicriso* because it has no nectar'. Ballini is still making it, though it wasn't available the last time I visited.

PECORINO, FICHI E MIELE DI CASTAGNO
PECORINO, FIGS & CHESTNUT HONEY

Cut a wedge of aged ewe's milk cheese into slices and a handful of ripe autumn figs in half. Serve with chestnut honey and a glass of fine red wine.

Salvatore e Giovanni Cannas

Salvatore Cannas has been a shepherd since he was 6 years old. He certainly doesn't look 70. What he looks is strong – not weightlifter strong, but vital and alive – like an advertisement for the benefits of a life spent outdoors among hills and fields and animals. 'My father never wanted me to leave Sardinia,' he says, unlatching a metal gate and skirting aside to let a flood of sheep stream into the barn for the first of their twice-daily milking. 'He thought we had enough – around 300 sheep, a bit of land, a decent living.'

The idea of personal space doesn't seem to have occurred to the sheep, who, except for the few stragglers and lambs frolicking at the edges, seem to move as one dreadlocked, bleating, multi-legged beast. Another gate snaps open and the first animals into the barn obediently march themselves into the milking room, duck their heads into the feeding trough, and proffer their teats to the milkman. 'I asked my father to come with me,' his voice booms over the din of animal and machine, as loud as his hands are large. 'He wouldn't even consider it.'

We step out of the barn and back into the blinding spring morning. The Cannas farm, Podere Lischeto, sits on an extraordinary spot – pastoral and dramatic all at

once. The contours of the hills in this part of Tuscany are strangely otherworldly, as if the earth here were subject to different geological forces than the rest of the planet. I first saw the farm in winter when the fields were ploughed and bare. In places, it looked as if the land had collapsed in upon itself like a fallen soufflé. It is a windblown, mostly treeless landscape that spreads out like a great bowl beneath the stone walls of Volterra. In spring, the farm takes on a bucolic dreaminess: pastures green with barley, oats and clover; big, cloud-filled skies; huddles of unshorn sheep crisscrossing the landscape; tinkle of bells; bleating of lambs.

'*È un miracolo di Gesù Cristo che ho avuto questo posto*,' says Salvatore. It does seem miraculous that a 26 year-old Sardinian shepherd, with only the modest flock of sheep that boarded the boat with him on his one-way passage to Rome, could end up with a sizeable organic cheese dairy, farm and *agriturismo* in the heart of *Toscana*.

It is a curious fact that most of the milk used to make Tuscany's favourite cheese, ewe's milk pecorino, comes from the flocks of local shepherds who aren't Tuscan at all, but Sardinian. They arrived in Tuscany in the 1960's, when the countryside had been virtually abandoned by farmers enticed away from their land by the bright lights of cities and industry. Farmland cost a pittance; farmhouses (the same ones that cost a fortune today) were thrown in as part of the bargain. Many of those shepherds never left. They married, raised families and became, if not quite Tuscan (no one becomes Tuscan simply by moving here, and anyway a Sardinian wouldn't want to), then – like Salvatore Cannas – enmeshed in the fabric of the place.

* * *

I'd known that Salvatore's Tuscan-born son Giovanni was a cheesemaker – the reputation of his organic pecorino brought me to Lischeto in the first place – but I didn't know that he never intended to become a *casaro*. 'I was a shepherd for a while in my teens, but that's hard work when you're young,' he explains, as we walk from the barn to the dairy. 'Never a day off. Always having to be up at dawn.' Giovanni has one of those compelling faces whose features add up to considerably more than the sum of their parts: heavy black eyebrows, his father's imposing nose, greying hair tied into a tight ponytail, a smile that hints at melancholy. He could have been a character actor... or a mime.

'I like the idea of being a shepherd,' he says, pulling on white rubber boots and a cotton smock. 'It's more poetic, more philosophical. You have this bond with the animals – you know them one by one.' At this time of day the dairy is in a flurry of activity. A *casaro* pulls a high metal whisk through milky white curds in a metal vat. Another directs litres of whey gushing out of a plastic tube into tubs to be made into ricotta. A table is covered with rounds of freshly made cheese. In the next room someone washes the cottony grey mould off young cheeses. 'Mould is good,' Giovanni explains. 'It's the cheese expelling moisture. It can't be rushed and it can't be artificially suppressed without compromising the cheese.'

Why did he start making pecorino? 'It made me sad that my father had nothing to show for his work. A truck came every day and took away the milk. That was it.' As

a child, Giovanni watched his grandmother make cheese in a big copper pot. They would both lay their hands on the fresh round of cheese to 'help the whey in.' She told him he'd make a fine cheesemaker because he was blessed with *mani calde* – warm hands.

We follow Giovanni into the aging cellar – cool and musty with its neat rows of cheeses at various stages of maturation. 'I began by giving cheese away – often to discotheques on the coast. That's where I liked to spend my time in those days, so it seemed a good place to start.' Before long he was supplying pecorino to a whole stretch of coastal Tuscany. These days he seems more drawn to social causes, participating in both a prison rehabilitation programme and *la Fattoria Didattica*, inviting school children to the farm and supplying organic cheese for school lunches.

When he became serious about cheesemaking Giovanni convinced his father to go *biologico* (organic). 'At first I didn't want to,' says Salvatore, joining us in the courtyard. 'I'd always aimed for volume. But I knew that if I wanted Giovanni to be involved I had to give him a chance to do things his way.' He beams a paternal smile at his son, who receives it with a mixture of chagrin and appreciation. 'He was right though – the milk is better and so is the land.' All the forage for the animals is grown on the farm and the crops are rotated so the soil isn't depleted.

'*Rimanete a pranzo?*' We are invited to lunch and Giovanni adds two places to the 35 he's already set in the dining room of the *agriturismo*. He brings out a wooden board bearing homemade prosciutto and a selection of the cheeses we've just seen in the aging cellar.

The *Balze Volterrane*, whose rind has been rubbed with a layer of olive and oak ash has the grassy, not unpleasantly bitter undertones of the raw milk and wild artichoke rennet with which it is made. 'This is what good sheep's cheese used to taste like,' Giovanni explains. 'It's a flavour that's been lost with technology. For today's market

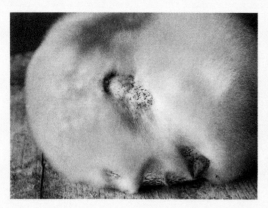

the taste is quite unusual. Not everyone likes it.' Podere Lischeto's pasteurised milk cheeses like *Rosso Volterrano* (*rosso* for the red tomato paste rubbed into its rind) are indeed smoother and more delicate. Different, not necessarily better or worse. Tuscan pecorino is never aged so long that it becomes a grating cheese (like pecorino romano), but the best are aged long enough to stand up to the finest Tuscan wines. Giovanni has us pay special attention to Lischeto's *Cacio del Monsignore*. The straw yellow cheese is aged for up to a year in old wine barrels filled with unhulled spelt. It has all the complexity of a raw milk cheese with a sharp, piquant bite at the end.

Along with the cheeses is a bowl of braised red peppers; a platter of tomatoes, spicy rocket and *baccellone* (a milky white, fresh pecorino); and a basket of broad beans still in their pods. A couple of words must be said about broad beans – known as *baccelli* in Tuscany and *fave* everywhere else. While the rest of the Mediterranean treats them a bit like peas, using them both fresh and dried but almost always cooked, Tuscans prefer to eat them young and tender, straight from the pod – together with a fresh round of pecorino made from the milk of sheep grazing on spring's first grasses. This pairing is not so much about flavour (fresh, tart and slightly bitter), as about the passage of time. Tuscans are rigorously faithful to the seasons. In winter they eat things like cabbage and squash. *Pecorino e baccelli* herald the arrival of spring.

Next come *gnudi* – 'naked' ravioli – or more precisely, ravioli without their pasta on. In most parts of Tuscany these are made with a combination of spinach and ricotta. Lischeto's kitchen uses only ricotta and the *gnudi* are soft, light little pillows covered with mutton *ragù*.

The *secondo* is lamb again, this time roasted, with bones so tiny I feel almost ashamed to eat it. Most of the time it is easy enough to forget the connection between what lives in the barn and what appears on the plate, to close an eye to the fact that we nourish ourselves with things that once were alive. But there is no sentimentality on a farm – even ones like Podere Lischeto. What there is in its place is something far more valuable: honesty, integrity and an abiding respect – not only for the bonds of family, but also for the welfare of the land and the creatures living upon it.

PEPERONATA
BRAISED RED PEPPERS

Halve, core and deseed 3 or 4 red peppers, then cut into long thick strips. Put them in a pan with a good splash of olive oil and sauté for a couple of minutes over a low heat. Add a little water, season with salt, then cover and cook over a gentle heat, stirring every so often until the peppers are soft but not mushy. Makes enough to serve 4.

PECORINO E BACCELLI
PECORINO & BROAD BEANS

Look for the freshest, most tender, early season broad beans you can get your hands on. Beans from wilted or dried out pods won't do. When you open them, the inside of the pods should be pale green and downy, and the beans not so big that you'd be tempted to peel them. Buy a wedge of fresh spring pecorino cheese. If you're feeling generous, shuck the beans into a bowl, cut the cheese into little pieces and dress with very good olive oil and a grinding of black pepper. Otherwise, simply put the beans and cheese on the table, along with a loaf of country bread and a carafe of young red wine, and let everyone help themselves.

GNUDI CON SUGO DI PECORA
'NAKED' RAVIOLI WITH MUTTON SAUCE

SERVES 6

for the sugo

8 tablespoons olive oil

500g lean mutton, minced

1 mutton bone

1 small onion, finely chopped

1 carrot, finely chopped

1 celery stalk, finely chopped

10 juniper berries

2 bay leaves

small glass of Vin Santo or other dessert wine

sea salt and freshly ground black pepper

2 garlic cloves, crushed

1 rosemary sprig, leaves only, finely chopped

for the gnudi

500g sheep's milk ricotta

125g aged pecorino or parmesan, freshly grated, plus extra to serve

2 large eggs, lightly beaten

3 tablespoons fine breadcrumbs, plus extra if needed

pinch of freshly ground nutmeg

sea salt and freshly ground white pepper

flour for dusting

To prepare the sugo, warm half the olive oil in a saucepan, then add the mince, mutton bone, vegetables, juniper berries and bay leaves. Sauté for 10 minutes, stirring often. Pour in the wine and continue cooking until the alcohol has evaporated, the vegetables are softened and the meat is brown. Add a bit of water if necessary, to avoid sticking.

Stir in 500ml water and season well with salt and pepper. Bring to a simmer and cook, covered, for 3 hours, adding more water if the sauce begin to dry out. Remove the mutton bone and bay leaves, then pass the sauce through a mouli (food mill), or mash with a fork.

Heat the remaining olive oil in a small saucepan, add the garlic and rosemary and sauté until the garlic is golden. Remove the garlic, then stir the aromatic oil into the sauce.

To make the gnudi, put the ricotta in a muslin-lined sieve and leave to drain for 20 minutes. Tip the ricotta into a bowl and add the grated cheese, eggs and breadcrumbs. Season with nutmeg, salt and white pepper, and combine well with a wooden spoon. The mixture should form a thick paste – if it's at all watery, stir in a tablespoon or two of additional breadcrumbs.

Lightly flour your work surface and your hands. Shape the gnudi by rolling the paste into 2cm balls and dust each lightly with flour. Bring a large pot of water to the boil and add salt. Drop the gnudi into the pan and boil until they float to the surface, about 3 minutes. Scoop them out with a slotted skimmer and ladle into individual bowls.

Spoon the sauce over the gnudi and serve with grated pecorino or parmesan.

Massimo Biagi

Chilli Collector

'*Guarda*,' says Massimo Biagi, pointing to the lipstick red pods dangling like shiny lanterns from the branches of a leafy green plant. 'They just beg to be eaten.' He picks one carefully where the stem meets the branch and makes a nest for it in his open palm. 'You'd think it was a fruit.' You might just… until 7 or 8 seconds after biting into it, when you'd morph into a cartoon character: mouth on fire, smoke billowing from your ears, frantically searching for a way to quench the flames. Water won't work; alcohol, salt or something acidic like a tomato will help… a bit.

'Funny thing is,' he says with a wry smile, 'as soon as your mouth had cooled down, you'd be back for more.' Like moths to a flame. Such is the allure of the habanero – the world's hottest chilli and Biagi's favourite, which is saying something considering that he has over 800 in his collection of *peperoncino* cultivars.

Biagi is known in chilli loving circles as the Pepper Professor, though he describes himself as a 'technical officer responsible for the University of Pisa's hybrid research greenhouses.' He looks a bit like a benevolent character from a Dr. Seuss book: deep

smile lines around the eyes, a Yertle-the-Turtle nose, thick grey brush of a moustache and the general air of someone who knows how to have a laugh.

He slices the habanero down the middle, exposing a womb-like heart packed with pale seeds, and holds it under my nose. Hints of apricot, smoke and flowers mingle with the familiar scent of sweet peppers. My throat tightens and eyes prick just from smelling it. 'They don't lose their flavour when you cook them,' he explains. 'Once you've eaten an *aglio, olio e peperoncino* made with habanero, you'll never make it with anything else.' Spaghetti tossed with olive oil, garlic and *peperoncino* (which in Tuscany is sometimes called *zenzero*) is the quintessential Italian meal-of-first-resort on those tricky occasions when one finds oneself with a houseful of people to feed and an empty cupboard. No Italian kitchen is ever without those four basic ingredients, and everyone loves *una bella spaghettata*.

'We're attracted to *peperoncini*,' says Biagi, explaining away our apparent masochism, 'because capsaicin (the chemical compound responsible for giving chillies their heat) stimulates our bodies to release endorphins – just like eating chocolate, having sex or running a marathon does!' *Peperoncini*, Biagi argues, do more than simply exalt the flavour of the most humble foods: they make us feel good.

We leave the habanero and follow Biagi up and down the chilli beds he's cultivated on a bit of borrowed land outside the seaside town of Torre del Lago. Row upon row of meticulously tended plants are at various stages of flowering and fruiting. 'A green chilli is an unripe chilli,' he tells us. 'Spicy, but grassy tasting, rather than sweet.' He shudders at the thought. All chillies, it seems, turn colour as they mature, going from green to black then through to red, orange or yellow.

Alongside all the usual suspects – cayennes, jalepeños, serranos – Biagi points out wild Amazonian chillies; killingly fiery Peruvian ajis; chillies shaped like nipples, like cherry tomatoes; variegated chillies; chillies from China, Africa, India, Central America. An infinity of chillies… and all very interesting, fascinating even, but what I find myself really wanting to know is what compelled Biagi to start collecting in the first place.

* * *

'Back in 1995, I was hybridising pelargoniums (geraniums) for a friend. She said that if I could make her a yellow geranium, she'd buy me a villa in the Bahamas.' He stops before a plant laden with slender red, devilishly pointed *peperoncini*. 'Well… I couldn't, but one day I was having lunch at her house – we ate *zuppa di ceci* – a perfectly ordinary chickpea soup, except that she put a little dish of these on the table,' he says, pulling a chilli off the plant. 'Peruvian aji. I watched everyone chop the chillies into tiny pieces and sprinkle them on their soup, so I did the same.'

The rest, as they say, is history. The friend gave him two fresh chillies and he planted their seeds. So began his collection. 'I wrote to a habanero farmer in the Yucatan and he sent me seeds and a fantastic handwritten letter in Spanish.' Biagi was hooked. He traded seeds, played at hybridising, and his collection grew in leaps and bounds.

'How do you make a hybrid?' I ask. '*È facile.*' Sure it is. '*Veramente facile,*' he insists, '*e divertente.*' Really easy, and fun. 'It's like inventing… only you're never sure exactly what you're inventing.' He picks up two plants and points out the tight white fists of their unopened blossoms. '*Si fa così.* First isolate a fully closed bud on each plant; when the buds open, manually cross pollinate the flowers with a toothpick; harvest the seeds from the resulting chilli (which will look the same as the other chillies on the plant); plant those seeds the next year and see what you get.'

There's something curious about those who've found an all-consuming passion in something the rest of us hardly give a thought to. 'Who do *peperoncino aficionados* fraternise with?' I wonder. Other *peperoncino* lovers, of course, and there are more of those than you might imagine. For starters, there's the *Accademia Italiana del Peperoncino*, with 5,000 members, its own glossy magazine, and an annual 5-day Peperoncino Festival in Calabria. Biagi will be there – with 250 *peperoncino* cultivars in tow. There are the De Bondt's, artisan chocolatiers in Pisa, who make bittersweet chocolates laced with smoked jalapeños and candied habaneros. Best of all, there are the *Monaci di Siloe*, a newly minted order of Benedictine monks who pray, study and grow *peperoncini* on a windswept hilltop in southern Tuscany.

Brother Roberto, Siloe's head gardener, explained the motivation behind the order's decision to cultivate chillies. 'We have olive trees. We were looking for something else to grow – not for commercial purposes, but as another way to put the land to good use and connect ourselves to the natural world.' Biagi is so inspired by the monks' enthusiasm, he's set out to create their very own cultivar: *lo zenzerino di Siloe.*

SPAGHETTI AGLIO,
OLIO E PEPERONCINO

SPAGHETTI WITH GARLIC, OLIVE OIL & CHILLI

SERVES 6

3 garlic cloves, crushed

5 tablespoons olive oil

2 fresh or dried chillies, finely chopped with their seeds

500g dried spaghetti

sea salt

finely chopped flat-leaf parsley to serve

Warm the garlic and olive oil in a large heavy-based frying pan over a low heat. When the garlic is blonde and fragrant, add the chopped chillies and remove the pan from the heat.

Boil the spaghetti in abundant salted water. Drain after about 8 minutes, when it is almost, but not quite cooked. Add the pasta to the pan with the seasoned oil and toss well over a high heat for a couple of minutes, until the pasta is al dente. Sprinkle with chopped parsley and serve.

OLIO AROMATIZZATO CON
AGLIO, PEPERONCINO E
BASILICO

GARLIC, CHILLI & BASIL MARINADE

Pour 250ml olive oil into a small bowl. Add 3 freshly chopped chillies with their seeds, 2 sliced garlic cloves, a handful of torn basil leaves and salt to taste. Let the mixture macerate for a couple of hours, then use as a marinade for grilled summer vegetables, such as aubergines and courgettes. Brush the grilled vegetables with the flavoured oil and leave them to stand at room temperature for an hour or so before serving.

ZUPPA DI CECI
CHICKPEA SOUP

SERVES 4

400g dried chickpeas, soaked in cold water overnight

sea salt and freshly ground black pepper

2 tablespoons tomato purée

4 tablespoons olive oil

50g pancetta, chopped

1 yellow onion, finely chopped

1 carrot, finely chopped

1 celery stalk, finely chopped

1 garlic clove, crushed

1 tender rosemary sprig, finely chopped

500g Swiss chard, cut into strips

to serve

extra-virgin olive oil to drizzle

4 fresh chillies, chopped with their seeds

Drain the chickpeas and place in a large cooking pot. Add 2 litres cold water and bring to the boil. Reduce the heat to a gentle simmer and cook for about 2 hours until the chickpeas are tender. Add salt towards the end of the cooking time.

Take out half of the chickpeas and pass them though a mouli (food mill) or purée in a blender and return to the pot. Stir in the tomato purée.

In a separate pan, warm the olive oil over a low heat, then add the pancetta, onion, carrot, celery, garlic and rosemary. Cook, stirring from time to time, until the vegetables are soft and fragrant.

Add the vegetable mixture to the pot of beans with the chard and season with salt and pepper. Simmer for approximately 30 minutes.

Ladle the soup into warm bowls. Offer olive oil and chopped chillies at the table.

POLLO SCHIACCIATO AL LIMONE E PEPERONCINO
FLATTENED SPICY LEMON CHICKEN

SERVES 4–6

1 roasting chicken, about 2kg, neck and giblets removed

250ml olive oil

juice of 1 lemon

4 fresh chillies, chopped with their seeds

sea salt

Lay the chicken on its back and cut down the centre of the breastbone. Turn it over and flatten, breaking the backbone and loosening the joints with the heel of your hand.

Whisk together the olive oil, lemon juice and chillies in a small bowl and season with salt. Lay the chicken flat in a shallow roasting pan and brush all over with the marinade. Pour any remaining marinade over the top and refrigerate for 2 hours.

Preheat the oven to 200°C/Gas 6. Roast the chicken, skin side up, for 50 minutes, basting regularly with the pan juices. Turn the oven down to 180°C/Gas 4 and continue roasting, basting more often, for a further 20 minutes or until the chicken is cooked. To test, insert a skewer into the thickest part of the thigh – the juices should run clear, not pink. Rest for 10 minutes before carving or cutting into serving pieces.

Cooperativa Agricola Paterna

Organic Farming Cooperative

'Don't even ask me about *zolfini*,' says Marco Noferi. We are standing in front of an enormous hearth watching a thick, glass flask of beans simmer beside the embers of a dying fire. '*Non ne posso più di questo fagiolo.*' Marco's had a belly full of the Arno valley's celebrated white bean, which is actually not so much white as a pale, greenish-yellow – the colour of *zolfo* (sulphur), from which it takes its name.

Still, it seems an odd thing for him to say. Marco's considered one of the *zolfino*'s original champions. He and 15 other friends started up the Paterna organic cooperative in 1977 on 20 hectares of tired farmland, hoping to repair some of the damage inflicted on the countryside when agro-business nosed its way into traditional farming, peddling chemical fertilisers, pesticides and the promise of higher crop yields. The *zolfino* seemed a perfect niche crop for small local farmers wanting to do right by the land – indigenous to the area; good for the soil (like all legumes, it fixes nitrogen); and happiest drinking nothing but rainwater.

The first time I drove out to Paterna to meet Marco, the *zolfino* was practically all we talked about: its lovely plumpness; the delicacy of its skin (which all but disappears upon cooking); its creamy texture; its incomparable flavour. But that was 7 years ago. A lot can happen in 7 years.

'The whole thing's gotten out of control,' he says, furrowing thick black brows that loom over his eyes like thunderheads. These days more than one farmer has put a locked fence around his *zolfino* patch – and not to keep the cows out. The *zolfino*'s become the talk of Tuscany, latest in a long line of pet products fawned over by gastronomes. The going price for a kilo of the dried beans this year is 28 euros – more than the cost of a fine cut of beef, and more than a little ironic, since the white bean has always been considered the poor man's meat around here.

The fact that Marco sees the *zolfino*'s revival as something of a failed experiment doesn't stop him from cooking them for our lunch. His quarrel is not with the bean, but with the way it's being exploited. I, for one, am happy to watch the spectacle of *fagioli* bubbling away in a flask by the fire – an experience which feels a bit like the gastronomic equivalent of glimpsing an endangered species in the wild.

Hardly anyone cooks beans this way anymore. Now there are cookers with gas hobs. There is affluence. Wine comes in tall slim bottles instead of potbellied flasks. But it wasn't so long ago that farmhouses were heated by massive fireplaces and supper was little more than *pane e companatico* – bread and something to go with the bread. Often that something was *fagioli*.

The beans were dropped *uno per uno* (there's no quicker way) into an empty *fiasco di vino* stripped of its straw and then covered with water. A couple of unpeeled cloves of garlic and a sprig of sage were pushed through the bottleneck along with a few black peppercorns, a sprinkling of salt and a splash of olive oil. A loose wad of flax was stuffed into the neck for a seal. Before bedtime, the bottle was placed on a bed of ashes and surrounded by the embers of the waning fire.

All through the night the beans simmered. *Piano, piano.* Slowly, slowly. By morning they were perfectly cooked – their interiors soft but not mushy, their skins still intact, the scene itself an emblem of everything we (and by we, I mean we non-Tuscans) love most about the food, about this place. Where else can resourcefulness, frugality, beauty and flavour peacefully inhabit the same humble flask?

* * *

We followed Marco to a shady pergola near the makeshift kitchen where Tamara Scarpellini, a co-op partner since 1985, had prepared lunch. He shook the steaming beans into a bowl and opened a bottle of Paterna Chianti. Viviano Venturi arrived with tomatoes and basil from his *orto*, and a heavy loaf of unsalted bread from his brother's wood burning oven. The last time I'd seen him, he was still a part of the Paterna cooperative. These days, he and his wife make organic jams and sauces from their homegrown fruits and vegetables, canning them under the label Radici.

Our meal consisted of four different dishes, though each was made with some combination of primary ingredients from the same short list: tomatoes, beans, olive oil, basil and bread (some of which was intentionally stale). I'd hovered over Tamara in Paterna's cramped kitchen while she cut open a few ripe tomatoes and rubbed them over untoasted bread, the juice seeping into the thick slices like seawater into sand. Then she doused the bread with olive oil and sprinkled it with salt. Stained red and speckled with seeds, *pane al pomodoro* did not, in truth, look all that promising. Shouldn't she have toasted the bread? Rubbed it with garlic? What about basil? And why don't we get to eat the tomatoes? I kept quiet. We were guests. It was a simple farmhouse lunch. What did I expect?

Tamara's bread salad was equally Spartan. 'People will put anything in a *panzanella* these days,' she said, whacking half a loaf of stale bread into pieces and soaking them in cold water until they came back to life – sodden, but springy and textured as wet sponges. '*Capperi, tonno, olive…*' She wrung the lumpish pieces out in handfuls, crumbling them into a bowl along with slivers of red onion and a handful of basil leaves torn into pieces. She approves of the addition of tomatoes and cucumbers, but not today. 'With bread this good, basil and onion are enough.' She dressed the salad with olive oil and wine vinegar and tossed it with her hands.

We ate almost in silence for the first few minutes, absorbed in the pleasure of the meal. Marco poured wine. We ladled out beans and drizzled them with more olive oil. Viviano sliced a half-kilo *cuore di bue* tomato into sections. It looked like a calf's heart – purply, wet and silky – and tasted of summer. There was an abundance at the table that had nothing to do with excess. The bread didn't need to be toasted. It had flavour enough, just as it was.

What conversation there was meandered with pleasant aimlessness – until we touched on the topic of *la campagna*. The countryside. '*La campagna è morta*,' Marco announced resolutely. He reminded me of Nietzsche proclaiming 'God is dead.' And

he had our attention. Despite the warmth of his welcome and his easy laughter, Marco can be unintentionally intimidating. I noticed this about him when we first met. He is fiercely intelligent, but never acts even remotely superior or condescending – and he'll treat you as an intellectual equal, even if you suspect that you are not.

'What do you mean?' I protested. The wine and oil on our table came from grapes and olives grown on this very land. The countryside might not be all it once was, but surely it is alive. 'The days of family farming are over,' he answered. True. Rare are the *contadini* who still live off their land, content to subsist on a few acres, a few animals, and a good measure of frugality.

'Agriculture in Tuscany has entered the post-modern phase.' The words would have sounded dry and ominous if Marco's delivery hadn't been so relaxed. He pulled a pack of cigarettes from his pocket, lit one and leaned back in his chair. 'The issues are changing. Seeds are in the hands of multinationals. There's a water crisis. Global warming. *Zolfini* beans and village *sagre* celebrating traditional foods are a farce if we don't look honestly at the real issues facing agriculture.' He's tired of dinner parties where everyone oohs and ahhs over the latest gastronomic trend. 'People are eating with their heads. There's too much chat.' Food has become fashionable.

Post-modernism isn't necessarily a problem, according to Marco. 'The trouble is when people romanticise the past,' he said, looking me squarely in the eye. 'Traditional farmers were also a conservative and closed-minded lot. We shouldn't be afraid of the future.'

But what sort of future? Marco shrugged. 'How should I know?' He might not know, but there are few people whose opinion on the subject I value more. '*Va bene*,' he said, straightening up in his chair. 'For one thing, we should give more attention to the producer than to the product. Our baker buys his flour locally, but the wheat comes from Canada. This shouldn't happen. We should rethink the food distribution chain – localise production to create a direct rapport between the product and the consumer.' But that's not enough. What Marco would really like to see is a shift in consciousness. 'Tradition and sentimentality aren't our bridge to the past. We need to have respect for what we eat – a measure of sobriety, and a sense of the sacred in our relationship with food.'

The day unravelled as the sun poured its heat on the fields and we lazed in the shade of the arbour. Viviano brought a pot of espresso to the table and we variously stirred sugar into the small metal cups or downed our thimblefuls of thick muddy brew in one fell swallow. It's not easy to reconcile Marco's unflinching gaze towards the future with the bucolic reality of our lunch on the farm. 'And so what,' I think he'd have said if I told him so. That is the challenge.

PANZANELLA
BREAD SALAD

SERVES 4

6 thick slices day-old, course-crumbed country
bread (preferably unsalted)
1 sweet red onion, halved and thinly sliced
2 generous handfuls of basil leaves, torn
60ml olive oil, more or less
drizzle of red wine vinegar, to taste
sea salt and freshly ground black pepper

Soak the bread slices in a bowl of cold water for
10–15 minutes. Drain, then squeeze, a handful at
a time, to remove as much water as you can. Rub
the bread between your hands, crumbling it into a
large salad bowl.

Add the red onion and torn basil leaves, then dress
with olive oil, wine vinegar, salt and pepper, tossing
well with your hands.

FAGIOLI AL FIASCO
BEANS IN A FLASK

For these you need both a fireplace and a wine flask – neither standard items in most households. On that rare occasion when you happen to find yourself with both…

In the early evening, light a wood fire in the hearth. Peel the straw from a 1.5 litre glass wine flask and fill the flask with 300g dried Tuscan white beans, 3 unpeeled garlic cloves, a sprig of sage leaves, a few black peppercorns and a pinch of salt. Pour in half a glass of olive oil and fill the flask to just below the neck with water. Make a stopper with a wad of flax, and tie the stopper to the neck of the bottle to keep it from falling in. Before you go to bed, set the flask in the centre of a pile of ashes and embers near the dying fire. At lunchtime the next day, shake the beans out of the flask into a bowl. Makes enough to serve 4.

SALSICCE E FAGIOLI ALL'UCCELLETTO
SAUSAGES & WHITE BEANS IN TOMATO SAUCE

SERVES 4

for the beans

400g dried cannellini beans, soaked in cold water overnight (see note)

2 tablespoons olive oil

2 garlic cloves, unpeeled

4–5 sage leaves

few black peppercorns

sea salt

for the sausages

4 garlic cloves, crushed

2 tablespoons olive oil

6 fresh Italian sausages

400g can Italian plum tomatoes, drained

4–5 sage leaves

pinch of dried red chilli flakes

Drain the beans and place in a heavy-based cooking pot with 2 litres water, the olive oil, garlic, sage and peppercorns. Bring to a simmer. Cover and simmer over a low heat until tender, about 2 hours. Salt the beans three-quarters of the way through the cooking time.

To cook the sausages, warm the garlic and olive oil in a large heavy-based frying pan until the garlic is golden. Add the sausages and cook, turning, until lightly browned on all sides, then break them up in the pan with a wooden spoon. Drain the beans, reserving 120ml of the liquor.

Add the tomatoes, sage and chilli to the sausage with the reserved liquor and simmer for 5 minutes, breaking the tomatoes up with a wooden spoon. Add the beans and continue simmering for about 15 minutes until the sausages are cooked and the sauce has thickened, stirring carefully from time to time so as not to break up the beans. Check the seasoning and serve.

Note If you are able to find fresh cannellini beans, use them for this recipe: you will need 1kg fresh beans in their pods. You won't need to soak them overnight and they will cook in about 45 minutes.

PANE E POMODORO
BREAD & TOMATO

Cut a ripe summer tomato down the middle and rub it over the top of a thick slice of good country bread – naturally leavened and baked in a wood burning oven is best. Pour on some extra-virgin olive oil and sprinkle with salt and basil leaves.

Fausto Guadagni

Lardo di Colonnata Producer

Fausto Guadagni has worn himself out in a decade long battle that he sometimes feels like he's winning and losing at the same time. It's not easy taking on the European Community, the corporate food distribution network and Italy's bureaucratic machine from a tiny, end-of-the-road village in the Apuane mountains.

Beware of those who would have you believe that this is little more than a fight about preserved pork fat (to be precise, the fat off the back of a well fed pig). Guadagni will tell you that it is about honesty, about the honouring of traditions and about the education of a public prey to gastro-profiteers looking to cash in on a hot 'new' product. *Lardo di Colonnata*, the product in question, has in fact been a staple food of his village Colonnata since Roman times.

* * *

From a distance, the jagged cliffs of the Apuane look snow capped, even in summer. But they aren't. They are made of stone – pale grey Carrara marble, the same stuff that Michelangelo used to sculpt the David. The truth is that *marmo di Carrara* doesn't come from Carrara at all, but from quarries high in the mountains above it. Every day trucks rumble down dusty switchbacks loaded with rough blocks of stone destined for all parts of the globe. The village of Colonnata sits in the midst of it all, clinging to the steep edge of a mountain, one side facing the scarred landscape of the mines, the other overlooking woodlands covered in chestnut, oak and beech.

'There wasn't even a road going up to Colonnata until the 1950's,' Guadagni tells me, scraping clean the creamy white edges of a chunk of *lardo* he's just removed from the *conca* (marble tub) where it has spent the last 6 months soaking in a salty brine seasoned with pepper, garlic and over a dozen herbs and spices. 'There was no electricity and the marble was dragged down the mountain by oxen. Men didn't come to work for the day, but for a fortnight. They lived in the quarry and subsisted on bread and this,' he says piercing a corner of the slab of *lardo* with an official looking red plastic tag embossed with a European Community code. The tag identifies that the product comes from Guadagni's *larderia* in Colonnata. 'Finally an absolute guarantee of authenticity. Let's hope it is enough.'

Lardo di Colonnata's transformation from quarryman's elemental foodstuff to prized gastronomic delicacy is a cautionary tale. 'Before the road was put in, just about

every family in Colonnata made its own *lardo*,' Guadagni explains. 'With the road came a bit of tourism and an appreciation of the product. By the 1990's there were about a dozen of us selling it commercially.' Once *lardo di Colonnata* made a name for itself, it didn't take long for there to be suspiciously more of it on the market than could ever have been produced in the tiny village.

To the outrage of Colonnata, the government's first tactic was to go after the village's *lardo* producers. In the spring of 1996 police vans drove up to the town and put its *lardo* under house arrest, sealing the doors of the preserving cellars. Officials couldn't figure out what to do with a product that had no registered title, no formal list of ingredients, no artificial preservatives, no officially enunciated methodology in a Europe increasingly obsessed with regulating every comestible within its borders. 'What did they find after all their analyses?' exclaims Guadagni over lunch at his sister's restaurant Locandapuana across the street from his *larderia*, 'What we knew all along. No bacilli. Nothing pathogenic. Salt is an age old preservative; fine grain marble is a natural refrigerator – it absorbs the coolness of the cellar and maintains a stable temperature.'

Of course, once *lardo di Colonnata* was given a clean bill of health, everyone wanted in on the game. 'People wanted to make *lardo* in Carrara warehouses conveniently near the *autostrada*, instead of lost in the hills like us. They wanted to make it in 3 not 6 months, age it in refrigerators rather than marble cellars, and pump it with additives like nitrates.' At onerous personal expense (the bills have yet to be fully paid) Colonnata's *lardaioli* registered themselves as users of the name *lardo di Colonnata*. They hired a lawyer and petitioned local and European Community lawmakers to define *lardo di Colonnata* in accordance with its traditional place and manner of production – and to protect it with IGP status *(Indicazione Geografica Protetta)* so that only properly made *lardo* that really came from Colonnata could call itself such. In 2004 they succeeded and, more recently still, the Italian government instituted the stamp and seal requirement to insure traceability back to the source.

Guadagni is not entirely satisfied. 'It's easy enough for people to understand what goes into making *lardo di Colonnata* if they come up the mountain to see us,' he says. 'But how do you make the product understood in a European marketplace? Look at us. We're a tiny little village with a handful of producers. We don't have the resources to mount a full fledged information campaign.' Guadagni wants his product to reach an informed consumer, and believes that the European Community and the Italian Ministry of Agriculture should bear the burden of getting the good word out. 'As for me,' he says, 'I've had it with lawyers and bureaucracy. I just want to do my work.'

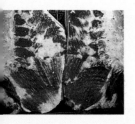

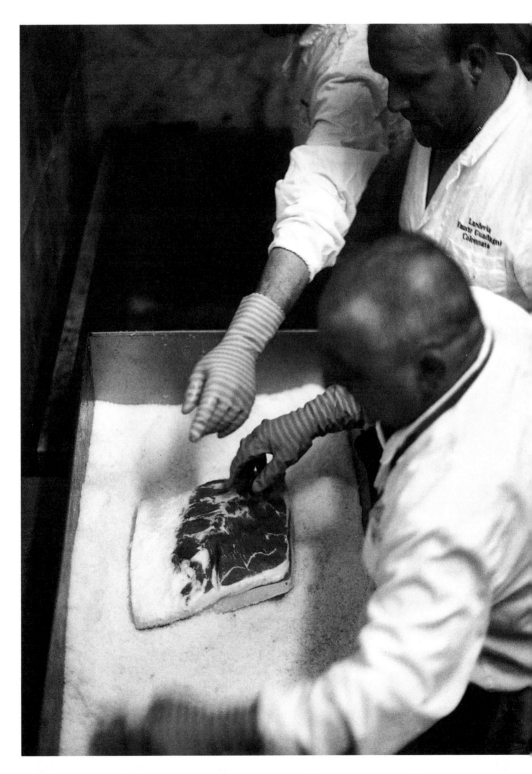

A LARDO PRIMER

How to make the real thing

Live in the village of Colonnata… preferably your family has for untold generations. Know that *lardo* is only cured during the relatively cool, wet months from September to May.

Procure one or more bathtub-sized marble *conche* (preserving tubs). Pale grey, fine-grain marble from the Canaloni quarry works best – large-grain is too porous for the brine; medium-grain marble is better for statuary.

Create an aging cellar or workroom for the *conche*, which benefits from Colonnata's unique microclimate – influenced by a combination of altitude, sunlight, sea breezes, surrounding woodland and humidity. Artificial refrigeration is not permitted.

Trim the meat off the fat from the back of a freshly slaughtered pig. Cut the fat into rectangular pieces and massage each piece with sea salt.

Rub the floor and walls of the *conca* thoroughly with fresh garlic.

Scatter the floor with a layer of salt and cover with a layer of mixed herbs and spices. Guadagni won't divulge the precise mixture he uses – 'every family has its own' – except to say that it contains the same 12 ingredients his father used and includes things like black pepper, cinnamon, nutmeg, cloves, star anise, marjoram, oregano and sage.

Cover with a layer of coarsely chopped garlic, followed by a layer of rosemary leaves.

Lay the lard into the *conca* as if you were tiling a floor. No overlaps, no empty spaces.

Continue layering with salt, spices, garlic and rosemary until the conca is full.

Cover the tub and leave for 6 months, checking occasionally to correct the brine if it is too wet or dry.

How it should look and taste

COLOUR: Pale, pinkish-brown, covered with a dark layer of salt, garlic and spice mixture.

SCENT: Wonderfully fresh, fragrant and redolent of herbs and spices; not like rancid old fat.

FLAVOUR: Delicately savoury and ever so faintly sweet at the same time.

GUADAGNI'S TASTE TEST: 'Try it on its own – without bread or wine – and most importantly, at blood temperature. Anything's palatable that's thinly sliced, seasoned with herbs and served on warm toast. You can't pass off a fake at blood temperature. Put a slice in your mouth and let it melt. Common pork fat will ball up and be impossible to swallow. *Lardo di Colonnata* will simply dissolve. Your lips will feel moist, like they've been rubbed with cocoa butter.'

How to eat it

In the days when there was little more to eat than *pane e companatico* (bread and something to go with the bread), *lardo di Colonnata* was the quarryman's calorie rich *companatico* of necessity.

Traditionally it was cut into thin slices and draped over bread that was sometimes rubbed with tomato or otherwise accompanied by spring onions, salted anchovies, capers or wild, red-leafed oregano.

At her restaurant, Guadagni's sister Carla offers it as a starter, laying it out like pale pink ribbons on a plate and serving it with either traditional accoutrements, *panizza* (chickpea flour fritters), or more unusual pairings like white watermelon jam, or sweet fig and juniper berry 'salami.'

Carla Guadagni uses *lardo di Colonnata* like butter or oil when cooking – only you don't need as much. She cuts it into small dice to use for sautéeing aromatic vegetables at the start of a *ragù*, or dollops it on rabbit when making *coniglio lardellato*.

WINE: *Lardo di Colonnata* wants a crisp, young wine. Strong – up to 13 or 14% alcohol, but still fresh with fruit. Sparkling wines are good too. Complex barrel aged wines are too heavy.

Gionni Pruneti

Olive Oil, Saffron & Irises

There's a lot of hand-wringing among farmers of a certain age about who will take over the land once they retire. The general consensus among old-time *contadini* is that young people don't want to farm anymore. They're not up for the hard work – they'd rather be speeding around in fast cars, or talking on their mobile phones. 'No,' they sigh and shake their heads. 'Life's gotten too cushy for the next generation to put up with the rigours of farm life.'

Ask those same *contadini* about Gionni Pruneti, and if they've ever crossed his path, their weathered faces will sparkle with delight. '*Un bravo ragazzo.*' '*In gamba.*' '*Incredibile.*' Tuscans don't tend to dole out compliments gratuitously, nor (to over generalise) do they tend to abide much by innovation, and yet the lanky blond 27 year-old who farms organic olives, irises and saffron in the countryside around San Polo in Chianti garners nothing but praise from his elders.

'I've always loved this life,' says Gionni, raising his voice over the sound of a thousand ripe olives turning from fruit into oil. (His parents' Italianised spelling of 'Johnny' provoked such consternation at his christening that the family had to agree to enter a 'proper' Italian name in the parish baptismal records.) 'I used to pick olives with my *nonno* Natalino. Even when I was 8 years old, I'd sometimes spend the whole night in the *frantoio* when the olives were being pressed.' He still does, though these days it's every night during the 6 weeks or so it takes to bring in the olive harvest.

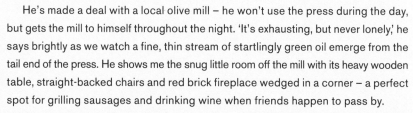

He's made a deal with a local olive mill – he won't use the press during the day, but gets the mill to himself throughout the night. 'It's exhausting, but never lonely,' he says brightly as we watch a fine, thin stream of startlingly green oil emerge from the tail end of the press. He shows me the snug little room off the mill with its heavy wooden table, straight-backed chairs and red brick fireplace wedged in a corner – a perfect spot for grilling sausages and drinking wine when friends happen to pass by.

To say that Gionni is the fourth generation of Pruneti's to farm the family land is true up to a point. His father Gilberto, son of Natalino, grandson of Girolomo (founder of the Pruneti farm), is well versed in the ways of the farm, 'as is anyone who was raised on a *fattoria*,' he insists, though he left farming to study to become a skilled mechanic. 'Those were the days when any family that could afford to take their kids off the farm to be educated did,' Gilberto explains.

'Everything I know about farming I learned from my grandfather,' Gionni says, picking up a bright green olive, crushing it between his palms and rubbing his hands together until the fruit's sticky juices give way to the fresh grassy smell of new oil. 'He was a sort of second father.' Gionni (who now collaborates with his brother Paolo) took over the Pruneti farm from Natalino when he was 20 years old. In a handful of years he has proven himself faithful to tradition, but not slavishly so; enthusiastic about innovation, but prudently so; and possessed of the singular genius that seems to come to those who thrill to their chosen work.

* * *

The first time I visited the Pruneti farm was in the spring when the town of San Polo in Chianti was abloom with irises. Slender green stalks with frilled papery flowers smelling of grapes and bubblegum sprouted from even the humblest front garden. White cotton banners painted with purple irises and announcing *La Festa del Gaggiolo* (the town's annual iris festival) hung from the windows of nearly every house. At the edge of town, the Pruneti's field of dew-tinged blossoms spreads over the countryside like an impressionist landscape.

The iris is the symbol of Florence, albiet somewhat confusingly so, since Florentines tend to refer to the stylised image as *il Giglio*, which in fact means 'lily'. Beautiful though it may be, it is not the flower that interests Gionni, but its ginger-like rootstock (orrisroot), which has the powdery scent of sweet violets and has been used for centuries in perfumes, powders and soaps, and as a remedy for snakebites, coughs and depression.

'Irises grow wild all over Tuscany,' Gionni explains. 'They love dry, stony soil – just like grapevines.' They also thrive at the edges of terraced fields or tracts of woodland, or on bits of farmland unsuitable for most crops. The town has been famous for iris production ever since the 1800's when its orrisroot was in great demand by perfumers in Grasse. Gionni hands me a yellowed photo of himself, aged about 5, cross-legged atop a mountain of dried orrisroot, an oversized straw hat perched on his head. These days, the Pruneti harvest goes straight to Florence's divine *Officina Farmaceutica di Santa Maria Novella*, the apothecary, perfumery and de facto temple to the senses founded in the 13th century by Dominican friars of the Santa Maria Novella church.

A few years ago Gionni decided to try his hand at cultivating another bloom: *Crocus sativus*, the hardy purple flower whose dried red stigmas are known and loved as saffron, the world's costliest spice. 'I noticed that every autumn when I'd look for mushrooms in the woods, or walk through an abandoned vegetable plot, I'd always come across a few crocuses,' he explains. The Pruneti's had always grown saffron crocuses for their own use.

I ask why saffron is so expensive when crocuses manage to grow without anyone actually tending them. Gionni hoots with laughter and patiently takes me through the mathematics. 'It takes 50 kilos of flowers to get 1 kilo of stigmas. Figure that a hectare

of land will produce somewhere around 10 to 15 kilos of stigmas. Once they're dried over oak embers, each kilo shrinks down to about 200 grams.'

I was further humbled when he went on to describe how the saffron is harvested. 'The crocuses usually begin blooming in October. We go out into the field early in the morning and pick the whole flowers,' he says. 'Then we empty our baskets in the work room and spend the rest of the day sitting around a table talking and plucking three red threads from every bloom.' The good news is that when it comes to *zafferano*, less really is more. A quarter gram of the spindly red filaments will flavour a dish for 6 to 8 people. And there's no sense showing off by adding an extra pinch. Too much saffron looses all its seductiveness and becomes ruinously bitter.

* * *

Of the farm's three main crops, olive oil is the Pruneti's lifeblood – hardly surprising, since without *olio di oliva* the Tuscan kitchen would grind to a halt. Rare is the farmhouse that doesn't have at least a few rows of gnarled, silvery-leafed olive trees in the garden, if the terrain and the climate will support them. Local farmers have always planted their olive groves with a variety of trees to help with cross-pollination, and their oil is traditionally a blend of the resulting olives. Tuscans who don't have their own olives usually buy their oil for the year from friends or neighbours who do and store it in 20 or 30 litre stainless steel containers. The average household will get through around a litre of *olio* a week.

In his approach to *olio di oliva*, Gionni manages to honour tradition while testing its boundaries. 'It is a personal challenge, ' he explains as he picks a shiny blue-black olive off a tree on the terraced hillside above the Pruneti farmhouse. 'I want to get the most out of this olive,' he tells me. 'Look at the tree. It's a *leccino*. You can tell by its long drooping branches and upturned tips.' He walks over to another tree, picks off a fruit and hands it to me. The colour's the same, but the olive is smaller and rounder than the *leccino* and the tree's branches are perky and upright. A *moraiolo*.

'You see,' he says excitedly. 'The *moraiolo* is sweet and mild, but has an intense aroma, a bit grassy in your mouth, but peppery on the throat. *Frantoio* olives are slightly bitter – astringent like raw artichokes. *Correggiolo* is forceful on the palate, but smooth down the throat.' Gionni is determined to identify the optimal growing, harvesting and pressing conditions for each individual variety, and bottle their oils both as traditional blends and select single variety oils. *Moraiolo* oil is fresh and fruity. Perfect, says Gionni, on boiled chickpeas, raw fennel, or even drizzled over dark chocolate cake. *Leccino* oil tastes greener, with the faint bitterness of sage and a hint of black pepper – Gionni's oil of choice for savoury pies and complex, spicy dishes.

'*Sono molto legato alla tradizione*,' Gionni explains. But he's not tied to tradition for tradition's sake. 'Farmers didn't used to stomp on grapes because it was traditional – it was just the best they could do at the time,' he says. 'Honouring tradition means remembering that we are artisans, not industrialists. Tradition is keeping our ties to the land. Sitting in a *tavola* for hours with friends. Listening to the old farmers tell their stories about how life used to be. It's remembering to be humble. Simple.'

PETTI DI POLLO ALLO ZAFFERANO
SAFFRON CHICKEN BREASTS

SERVES 4

350ml milk
1 scant teaspoon saffron threads
150g plain flour
sea salt and freshly ground black pepper
4 boneless chicken breasts, skinned
6 tablespoons olive oil
250ml white wine

Pour the milk into a small saucepan. Add the saffron threads and warm over a very low heat for 10 minutes. Set aside.

Season the flour with salt and pepper then use to coat the chicken breasts all over.

Heat the olive oil in a large frying pan. Add the chicken breasts and brown lightly on both sides.

Pour in the wine and let bubble until the alcohol has reduced, then pour the saffron-infused milk over the chicken. Continue cooking, turning occasionally, for about 20 minutes until the chicken breasts are cooked all the way through and the liquor has evaporated almost entirely.

PASTA FREDDA ALLO ZAFFERANO E POMODORI
PASTA SALAD WITH SAFFRON & TOMATOES

SERVES 6

1 scant teaspoon saffron threads
500g spaghetti or other dried pasta
sea salt
5 tablespoons olive oil, plus extra if needed
500g cherry tomatoes, halved
handful of basil leaves

Infuse the saffron threads for 15 minutes in 2 tablespoons hot water.

Boil the pasta in abundant salted water until it is almost al dente, but still slightly undercooked. Drain and transfer to a sauté pan.

Add the olive oil and infused saffron and toss over a high heat. Transfer to a serving bowl and leave to cool to room temperature.

Before serving, toss the pasta with the halved tomatoes and basil. Dress with additional olive oil if necessary.

CAVOLO NERO CON
LE FETTE
BRUSCHETTA WITH BLACK CABBAGE

SERVES 4

1kg cavolo nero or kale, ribs and stems removed

sea salt and freshly ground black pepper

8 slices country bread

3 garlic cloves, peeled

olive oil to drizzle

Cut the cabbage or kale into broad strips. Boil in a pot of salted water until wilted and tender, about 20 minutes. Drain. When it is cool enough to handle, squeeze out any excess water and roughly chop the leaves.

Toast the bread (over the embers of a fire is best, but the oven or toaster is fine too). Rub the toast with the garlic.

Spoon the cabbage on top of the toasts, season with salt and pepper, drizzle generously with olive oil and serve.

ZUPPA FRANTOIANA
OLIVE MILL SOUP

SERVES 6

200g dried borlotti or cranberry beans, soaked overnight in cold water

sea salt and freshly ground black pepper

4 tablespoons olive oil

1 red onion, finely chopped

1 carrot, finely chopped

1 celery stalk, finely chopped

500g cavalo nero or kale, ribs removed, leaves cut into strips

250g radicchio or chicory, coarsely chopped

200g butternut or acorn squash, cut into small chunks

2 potatoes, peeled and cut into small chunks

2 ripe tomatoes, peeled, deseeded and cut into chunks

pinch of fennel seeds

1 thyme sprig

to serve

6 slices day-old country bread

2 garlic cloves, peeled

best quality olive oil (freshly pressed if possible) to drizzle

Drain the beans and place in a large cooking pot with 2 litres water. Bring to the boil, then lower the heat and simmer, partially covered, until the beans are tender but not mushy, about 1½ hours. Season with salt towards the end of the cooking time.

Set aside a ladleful of beans. Pass the rest of the beans and the cooking liquid through a mouli (hand mill), or purée using a hand-held stick blender.

In a separate pan, warm 4 tablespoons olive oil. Add the onion, carrot and celery and cook over a medium heat until soft and fragrant, adding a bit of water to the pan from time to time to keep the vegetables from browning.

Add the puréed beans with their liquor and bring to a simmer. Add the cabbage or kale, radicchio or chicory, squash, potatoes and tomatoes. Add the fennel seeds and thyme, and season with salt and pepper. Simmer for 30 minutes, stirring in the reserved whole beans towards the end.

When ready to serve, toast the bread and lightly rub with the garlic. Lay a slice in each warm soup bowl. Ladle the soup on top, drizzle generously with olive oil and serve.

Mario Mariani

Terracotta

'Nothing much has changed here over the years.' Mario Mariani is using a long-handled pitchfork (and by long-handled I mean about 5 metres from top to bottom) to push a 50 kilo log to the back of the massive kiln he will spend 3 days bringing up to somewhere around 1000°C. 'The raw materials are still the same.' He puts down the fork and shows me two calloused hands. 'These,' he says, pausing as if to let me know that this first material is the most important, '*terra, acqua e fuoco.*' Earth, water and fire. Like his grandfather Anselmo and father Armeno before him, Mariani makes terracotta – or *cotto* as it is simply known in the town of Impruneta, where it has been famously made since the 14ᵗʰ century.

The ruddy orange, baked earth in its infinite forms is so much a part of the Tuscan vernacular that after a while you almost stop noticing it. Roofs are tiled with terracotta *tegole*. Beans are cooked in terracotta *cocci*. Geraniums spend their summers on terracotta terraces in terracotta pots. So do lemon trees. Winters here are too cold for them to survive outdoors, and since the renaissance Tuscany's grandest houses have overwintered their citrus trees in lovely glass-fronted *limonaie* (lemon houses).

Most beautiful of all are the waist-high terracotta urns called *orci*, traditionally used to store wine and olive oil. Two flank the door to Mariani's house, which adjoins the *cotto* works. One is dated 1617, the other 1651, and both bear the names of Impruneta, the town they came from, and Vanni – the potter who made them. Terracotta oil and wine urns are still fixtures in Tuscan country houses, the more mottled with age the better, though these days more of them are decorative than functional.

'The UCAS didn't like the old (lead-based) glazes that kept oil and wine from leaching through the *cotto*,' says Mariani, a propos of *orci*. UCAS? '*Ufficio Complicazione di Affari Semplici* – Office for the Complication of Simple Things.' His voice is laden with bemused disdain for bureaucratic meddling in activities, which thank-you-very-much, had been going along just fine for centuries without state intervention. He points to a large wooden crate bearing a Napa Valley, California address. 'This,' (non-toxically glazed *orcio*), 'is going to a California winemaker.' Here is a man who seems to be able to play by the rules even as he rails against them.

Mariani's kiln, workrooms and house are set back from a rutted road which leads up to the town's main square. A row of *orci* line one side of the drive; stacks of logs,

kindling and dry heather fill the other. The faded ochre façade is shaded by the wide limbs of an old tree, and the peal of church bells is distant enough to be both present and pleasant. It seems a good place to spend one's days. '*Io mi sono sempre divertito* – I've always had fun,' he says. 'I don't do this only for money, you know. You have to like this work to still do it by hand.'

'What exactly is involved in making terracotta by hand?' I ask Mariani. 'First you make the clay,' he answers. We walk round the back of the building to an excavation pit and a huge mound of grey earth, the surface of which has sprouted a few weedy flowers. It is difficult to reconcile its dull muddy colour with the warm hues of the *orci*. 'The iron in the soil expands during firing and turns from grey to red,' he explains.

Every summer Mariani moves a year's supply of earth, which has spent months drying out in the sun, to his 'soil warehouse' under the loggia. There it is milled as needed into a floury powder and then mixed (in what was once an industrial dough mixer) with water until it becomes a dense, tacky clay. Impruneta's tiles, vases, bricks and urns are particularly prized because the mineral content in the soil here produces a *cotto* that doesn't flake or crack in the cold. The terracotta vases in Florence's Boboli Gardens come from Impruneta. The bespoke *orci* in Rome's Quirinale (the presidential residence) were made by Mariani himself.

* * *

Several weeks later I return to find the workroom occupied by six half-finished *vasi da limoni* (lemon tree pots), their rims covered with light sheets of plastic to stop them drying out. They have been neither sculpted, nor thrown on a potter's wheel,

but built up from the ground freehand. Each sits on a square terracotta tile, which Mariani has used to delimit the boundaries of the pot's circular base.

The *vasi* are for a local noble family. Mariani has cast small round *borchie* (studs) of their family crest in clay to decorate the pots (and handily provide absolute proof of ownership). A box in the corner holds the rest of his cast plaster moulds: rosettes (for those of us without the privilege of title), the emblem of the *Repubblica Italiana*, monograms and more family crests.

Mariani motions me over to one of the pots. He ties an apron around his waist, fills a bucket with cold water, uncovers a wheelbarrow full of clay, and lights a thin, handmade *Toscano* cigar. The room is softly day-lit and everything in it but the cigar seems to be covered in a chalky grey layer of clay. He walks around the vase, tapping the rim with a wooden stick. He puts the *Toscano* in his mouth, dips his hands into the water and runs them along the upper edges of the vase; then he scoops up a mass of clay, massages it into a lumpish snake, and attaches it to the rim like a collar. He wets his hands again and begins to smooth and mould what I can now see is the vase's elegantly curved lip. He never stops moving, his arms and his torso pitched forward while his legs propel him in a slow backward dance round and round the pot.

A friend stops by to chat and watch him work. They speak in fits and starts about the health of various ailing family members, about Mario's blood sugar (a bit too high), peppering their dialogue with phrases like '*si va avanti; si fa quello che si può*' which loosely translates as 'one makes due' and aren't so much about resignation as they are about equanimity.

Mariani invites us over to the workshop for dinner the following Friday, which will be the third night after the next fire has been lit in the kiln. 'Bring your family,' he tells me. It's a tradition of Mariani's – feeding his friends when the kiln's at its hottest. 'Sometimes I've had 90 people in here eating *peposo*,' he tells me, referring to Impruneta's famous slow-cooked beef stew made with garlic, tomato, wine and black pepper – traditional potter's fare during firing time.

'Can I bring something?' 'No, no.' 'Who cooks, your wife?' '*Sono scapolo, cucino io*. I'm single, I cook.' 'Do people pay?' He laughs and looks at me as if it were the most commonplace thing to invite everyone you knew to supper once a month. I hardly know what to do with this sort of generosity, which doesn't even seem to recognise itself as such. 'What time?' I ask. 'Eight o'clock.' He answers. 'We'll be there.'

PEPOSO ALL'IMPRUNETINA
POTTER'S PEPPERY STEW

SERVES 6

1kg shin of beef

6 garlic cloves, crushed

130g tomato purée

1 tablespoon freshly ground black pepper

250ml red table wine

sea salt

Cut the beef into chunks and put into a large heavy-based flameproof casserole. Add the rest of the ingredients, seasoning with salt to taste, then pour in enough water to just barely cover the meat. Bring to a simmer over a low heat and simmer very, very gently, uncovered, for 3½ hours, stirring from time to time, until the meat is meltingly tender.

CROSTINI DI FEGATINI
DI POLLO
CHICKEN LIVER CROSTINI

SERVES 6

3 tablespoons extra-virgin olive oil

15g butter

1 medium white onion, finely chopped

350g chicken livers, trimmed and coarsely chopped

splash of Vin Santo or other sweet wine

2 salt-cured anchovy fillets, finely chopped

2 teaspoons brine-cured capers, drained and finely chopped

sea salt and freshly ground black pepper

1 long, thin loaf country bread, thinly sliced

Warm the olive oil and butter in a medium saucepan and sauté the onion over a low heat until it is soft and translucent, but not brown. Add the chicken livers and wine and cook gently, stirring frequently for 30 minutes, adding a bit of water to the pan if it dries out. Remove from the heat.

When the chicken livers are cool enough to handle, transfer them to a board and chop as finely as possible. Return to the pan and add the anchovies, capers and 250ml water. Season to taste with salt and pepper.

Bring to the boil, then lower the heat and simmer until the mixture has the consistency of a thick, moist sauce. Leave to cool slightly.

Lightly toast the bread slices and spread with the warm chicken liver mixture to serve.

INSALATA VERDE
GREEN SALAD

Tender lettuce leaves, the best quality extra-virgin Tuscan olive oil, sea salt and perhaps, but not necessarily, a tiny squeeze of lemon or a splash of wine vinegar are all that's needed for a simple *insalata verde*. Count on a couple of handfuls of leaves per person. Bitter lettuces like radicchio (they aren't always green) and peppery rocket are favourites. Any cutting lettuce is wonderful dressed this simply.

PESCHE AL VINO
PEACHES IN WINE

Pour a bottle of crisp white wine (nothing fancy, Vernaccia di San Gimignano works nicely) into a carafe or glass bowl. Peel, halve and stone 6 ripe white peaches, then cut the flesh into wedges and drop them into the wine. Cover and chill in the fridge for 2 hours or more. To serve, ladle the wine and peaches into goblets or shallow glass bowls. Serves 6.

Sergio Pollini

Tripe Vendor

They come even in the rain – mostly Florentines, predominantly (though not exclusively) men – to huddle around the steaming cauldrons on the back of Sergio Pollini's teal blue three-wheeled Ape (the iconic Italian hybrid that is equal parts scooter and truck) and eat tripe. Pollini has outfitted the cart well: metal arms unfold like wings to hold a canvas roof overhead; heavy sheets of plastic can be unrolled on either end to keep out the weather; a transistor radio is set to the sort of station that plays old Italian accordion tunes; and there are a few stools. Most people, however, choose to eat standing up at the counter. Plush it is not, but no one seems to mind. Florentines have always valued the ability to marry ingenuity and good food.

A silver-haired man in a green wool coat and hat strides up with a newspaper folded under his arm. '*Panino, bagnato sotto e sopra. Con sale e il pizzico.*' This is more of a statement than a question – and it is made by Pollini, who seems quite sure that the gentlemen wants boiled beef stomach splashed with chilli sauce and sprinkled with salt, and that he wants it in a bun that has been dipped in broth (rather than in a white plastic tub). The man nods and opens his newspaper.

Pollini looks at me and laughs. He wears a white apron and a roughish smile, calls his female customers '*amore*' and any man under 60 '*figliolo*' (son). '*I tuoi compatrioti non mangiano queste cose.*' This is true. My lot (and by that I mean Americans, though the same can be said about many others) don't usually eat this sort of thing. Florentines, on the other hand, operate on the presumption that most parts of an animal are worthy of our gastronomic attentions.

'There has been a *trippaio* (tripe vendor) on this spot ever since the early 1900's,' Pollini explains. He has been a tripe vendor for the past 10 years. Before that he sold clothes out of a stall at the San Lorenzo market. 'There are four or five of us selling tripe and *lampredotto* within the old walls of the city.' Locals always speak of Florence's ancient walls as if they still encircle the city intact, even though whole sections have long been replaced by boulevards. 'Nowhere else in Italy do you find tripe stands like this… nowhere else in Tuscany for that matter,' he says. '*È una cosa fiorentina.*' It's a Florentine thing.

Trippa is the milky white lining of any one of a ruminant's 'pre' stomachs (in this case beef); *lampredotto* (known as *abomaso* outside Florence) is the final stomach itself. Pollini sells both *croce* (smooth white blanket tripe) and *cuffia* (spongy honeycomb tripe) and cooks them into such local standards as *trippa alla fiorentina* (tripe stewed

with tomatoes and dusted with grated parmesan) and *insalata di trippa* (a salad of tripe dressed with olive oil and lemon). *Lampredotto* is something else entirely – mauve brown, crumpled like a handkerchief, yet silky in texture, with a mild (albeit ever so vaguely barnyard) flavour. He also sells *matrice* (boiled cow's uterus), which on this particular morning more than a few ladies have purchased to take home, cut up and dress with nothing more than lemon, salt and pepper.

Pollini lifts the lid off one of the pots. Pieces of *lampredotto* and *trippa* bubble around in a thick dark broth studded with bits of carrot, onion, celery and tomato. He scoops out a piece of *lampredotto*, lays it on a chopping board and slashes it into strips using two knives at once. In the space of about 20 seconds he slices a rosette of bread down the middle (crusty outside, soft of crumb), spears the halves with a long-handled fork and plunges them into the broth, then loads the bun with meat, gives it a sprinkling of salt and a splash of *salsa piccante*, wraps it up in paper, and hands it to the man in the green hat along with a plastic cup of red wine. The price of such deliciousness: less than 4 euros.

'We get every sort of customer – labourers, *nobili* (aristocrats), *casalinghe* (housewives), a few curious tourists… but mostly Florentines. Some people come almost every day.' *Panini al lampredotto* are always on the menu, but the one or two other cooked offerings vary according to the season and Pollini's whim. Today there is *lampredotto in zimino* (beef stomach cooked in the way cuttlefish usually are here in Florence – with tomato, *peperoncino* and chard). 'Tomorrow I'll make tripe with tomatoes and white beans. The day after, *chissà*?' Who knows? One thing's for sure – whatever it is will be infinitely preferable to those soggy slices of reheated pizza and cans of Coke the tourists call lunch.

LAMPREDOTTO IN ZIMINO
BEEF ABOMASUM WITH CHARD

SERVES 4

1kg Swiss chard, leaves and stems
sea salt and freshly ground black pepper
600g beef abomasum, from the 4th stomach of the ox (cleaned and boiled by your butcher)
3 tablespoons olive oil
3 garlic cloves, crushed
2 dried chillies, crushed
400g canned Italian plum tomatoes

Boil the chard in lightly salted water for 5 minutes, then drain well, reserving a ladleful of the cooking water. When cool enough to handle, roughly chop the leaves and stems.

Rinse the abomasum under cold running water, then cut into thin strips and set aside.

Warm the olive oil and garlic in a frying pan until the garlic is golden. Add the abomasum and chillies, and sauté over a medium heat for a couple of minutes. Now stir in the tomatoes, breaking them up in the pan with a wooden spoon. Cover and simmer for 40 minutes, stirring every so often.

Stir in the chard and the reserved cooking water. Season with salt and pepper to taste and simmer for 15 minutes before serving.

INSALATA DI TRIPPA
TRIPE SALAD

SERVES 4

400g veal honeycomb tripe (cleaned and boiled by your butcher)
1 small red onion, finely chopped
small bunch of flat-leaf parsley, chopped
100g brine-cured black olives, pitted
4 tablespoons olive oil
juice of ½ lemon
sea salt and freshly ground black pepper

Give the tripe a good rinse with cold water, then dry well and slice it into thin strips.

Toss the tripe with the red onion, parsley and olives in a salad bowl. Dress with olive oil and lemon juice, and season with salt and pepper to taste. Serve chilled or at room temperature.

Contini Bonacossi

Noble Winemaking Family

It is a Tuesday morning in late November and Countess Lisa Contini Bonacossi is expecting 30 people for lunch. Twin rows of cypress trees flank the steep drive up to the Villa di Capezzana like a formal invitation to a place both dreamlike and bewitching, its faded ochre walls and weathered statuary steeped in the patina of time. The grape harvest is long in and the vineyards are aflame in one final blaze of colour before the leaves fall from the vine and flutter lifelessly to the ground. It is the time of year when the sun seems to hover on the horizon and the countryside glows with golden light as if illuminated from within – the Tuscany of painters, postcards and poetry.

Patrizio Cirri, the family chef, is in one of the Capezzana winery's four kitchens preparing a meal that will begin with toasted bread doused with the estate's impossibly green new season olive oil and end with sweet thimblefuls of what is arguably the finest Vin Santo (Holy Wine) in all of Tuscany. In between there will be shallow bowls of creamy risotto studded with leeks and winter squash, veal stew with braised potatoes, and all manner of Capezzana wines – from 2 month-old, blushing pink Vin Ruspo to

Ghiaie della Furba, an opulent blend of Cabernet, Merlot and Syrah, poetically named after the Furba river which runs through the vineyard depositing pebbles in the soil.

For all its jaw-dropping, old-world splendour, the Capezzana estate is a hive of activity. Indomitably at its centre is the silver-haired, plain-spoken, 83 year-old *contessa*, who on this particular morning has just finished planting neat rows of tulip bulbs in the villa's formal garden, the only evidence of her labours the little mounds of earth where the soil has been disturbed. Her husband of more than 50 years, Count Ugo Contini Bonacossi is in one of the vineyards inspecting an irrigation pond he designed over the summer. Her son Filippo (youngest of seven) is across the road at the Capezzana *frantoio* (olive mill), overseeing the day's pressing and the delivery of olives picked from the estate's 25,000 trees. They arrive by the cartload, apple green or black as night. Beatrice ('Bea,' youngest daughter and most like her mother in temperament) is in the office on the phone to a foreign distributor. Bea's older sister Benedetta is dividing the morning between the *tinaia* (Capezzana's state-of-the-art fermentation cellar) and the dungeony 16th century aging cellar, which runs beneath the renaissance villa the Contini Bonacossi call home.

There is no shortage of wineries in Tuscany, but few can claim the lineage of Capezzana, which has been in the hands of the Contini Bonacossi since the 1920's. A parchment dated 804 A.D. reveals that vines and trees were cultivated for wine and olive oil at Capezzana as far back as the time of Charlemagne.

* * *

La contessa leads me across the villa's gravel courtyard to a rose garden improbably abloom so late in the year, picks a mandarin off the only tree not yet brought into the *limonaia* (lemon house) to overwinter, and offers it to me. 'I've got to plant 20 white rose bushes in the spring,' she says, her gravelly voice a trait that seems to be passed down through the female side of the family (the youngest of whom to have inherited it is her 11 year-old granddaughter Annalù). 'Sandra wants only white flowers.' The Contini Bonacossi's eldest daughter passed away this year and the *contessa* mentions her often, and always in the present tense.

Over coffee and orange-scented slices of Capezzana olive oil cake – made with spicy green new harvest oil rather than butter – she muses over the day she knocked on the servant's door of her future husband's summer home. 'My *nonna* Beatrice always invited all the grandchildren to spend the summer with her in Forte dei Marmi. There was one big room for the boys, another for the girls. The house was hidden in a pine grove, so we called it *la Pineta*.' She recalls the details as if they happened only yesterday, but in the telling the story sounds like a fairy tale. 'It was a Wednesday morning, market day, and I'd ridden my bicycle to the square with my sister. My tyres got caught in the tramway rails and I fell and scraped myself up. My sister brought me to Ugo's house.' She was 16, he was 18 – and he wasn't in, but she remembers *la Pineta* as her calling card and the day as her first introduction to the family.

A few years later, she was living in the Veneto with her parents. She'd studied chemistry in Padova, but the university had closed during the war. 'Ugo and two friends

showed up at our house in a tiny Fiat 500 on their way from Venice to Florence.' She impulsively decided to go back to Florence with them to continue her studies. They were married 18 months later. She finished her degree while raising their first three children and gave up an offer to work as a university research assistant only when she found out that she was pregnant again… with twins.

* * *

Conte Ugo walks into the room without noticing me, intent on the little posy of wild roses he's holding in both hands, and astonishingly dapper for his 85 years. '*Attenta*. They're full of thorns.' She takes the flowers by putting her hands over his and letting the soft undersides of the open petals rest in the bowl of her cupped palms. 'Did you pick them by the pond?' '*Sì.*' 'How was it?' 'Empty. But it'll be good when it rains.' It is a moment so sweet and full of intimacy I feel on the one hand like I've trespassed, and on the other inspired. There is surely nothing more romantic than a man picking wildflowers for his wife of half a century, when there's a garden full of old roses right outside his front door.

I hold out my hand and the count leans over and kisses it without kissing it, in a courtly gesture that for a moment leaves me feeling as if I too were part of some ancient aristocracy. 'Lori would like to see the Vin Santo rooms,' Lisa tells him, and he dutifully takes me off her hands as if there were nothing in the world he'd rather be doing.

We walk back into the courtyard, through the *limonaia* with its sheltered trees, smelling of nectar and bearing blossoms and fruit despite the chill, to an airy rectangular room whose windows are open to a cold northerly wind called the *tramontana*. It is like entering an enormous still life. Heavy bunches of Trebbiano, Malvasia and San Colombano grapes lay out to dry on rows of rush mats fitted into handmade bamboo racks. Technically the grapes are 'white' but visually they look warm and dusky, drenched in the sombre ochres of an Old Master oil painting. There they will stay until February when they will be vinified for 5 years in small *caratelli* (chestnut and oak casks).

The *vinsantaia* where the casks are left to age is surprisingly – and intentionally – unprotected from the vicissitudes of a climate where summers can be blisteringly hot and winters bone chilling. 'The fluctuation of temperature helps give Vin Santo its complexity of aroma and taste,' the count explains.

The amount of effort and time that goes into making Tuscany's favourite dessert wine explains why the ubiquitous cheap versions of the stuff which invariably appear at the end of a *trattoria* meal, along with a plate of dry almond *biscottini di Prato*, tend to be syrupy and uninspiring. The count is aghast at the notion of anyone dipping cookies into Capezzana's Vin Santo. 'It was recently ranked seventh among the top 100 wines,' he says. 'You wouldn't dip a cookie into a fine French wine, would you?'

'*Un buon Vin Santo è un vino da meditazione*,' he explains. This doesn't imply that one must meditate while enjoying it, simply that it is worthy of being savoured on its own. 'In Tuscany, if a friend comes over in the afternoon, you offer a small glass of good Vin Santo… not a cup of tea.' He glances discreetly at his watch and declares it to be lunchtime.

At the end of the deliciously long meal, the tables are cleared and a tray bearing tiny fluted goblets and a 375ml bottle of Vin Santo is set before us. The count pours us each a glass of the honeyed amber wine. 'I always say that winemaking is not immobile – it's like a ship that keeps moving ahead. We keep building on what we've learned.' He pauses and takes a delicate sip from his glass. 'But Vin Santo… it's like a statue. There's no way to improve it.'

RISOTTO CON PORRI E ZUCCA GIALLA
RISOTTO WITH LEEKS & WINTER SQUASH

SERVES 4

400g winter squash (butternut, acorn, kabocha or calabaza

2 leeks (white part only)

3 tablespoons extra-virgin olive oil

1.5 litres hot chicken or beef stock

1 teaspoon finely chopped flat-leaf parsley

60g butter

1 small yellow onion, finely chopped

450g arborio rice

60ml dry white wine

50g parmesan, freshly grated

Cut the squash into small cubes, discarding the skin and seeds; set aside.

Cut the leeks into julienne strips and place in a medium frying pan with the olive oil. Cook over a low heat until the leeks are soft but not browned, adding a splash of stock every few minutes to prevent them from burning.

After 10 minutes, add the squash and stir well. Cook over a low heat for 30 minutes, adding a little stock now and then to keep the vegetables moist.

At the end of the cooking time, stir in the chopped parsley and set the pan aside.

Keep the stock simmering gently in a pan on the back of the hob. Melt 40g butter in a medium, heavy-based saucepan. Add the onion and cook over a low heat until soft and transparent. Increase the heat to medium, add the rice and cook, stirring, for a minute until it is lightly toasted. Add the wine and let it evaporate.

Ladle just enough stock over the rice to cover it and cook, stirring, until most of the liquid has been absorbed. Continue adding the stock in small amounts as it is absorbed, stirring regularly. After about 15 minutes, when the rice is almost cooked, add the leek and squash mixture and stir well to combine. Continue cooking for a few more minutes, adding more stock if necessary. The risotto should be creamy but not runny.

Remove the pan from the heat and stir in the remaining butter and the grated parmesan. Let the risotto rest for a couple of minutes before serving.

SPEZZATINO ALLA CASALINGA
COUNTRY STYLE VEAL STEW

SERVES 4

750g boneless shoulder of veal

40g plain flour

6 tablespoons extra-virgin olive oil

1 small yellow onion, finely chopped

1 carrot, finely chopped

1 celery stalk, finely chopped

2 cloves, crushed

60ml red wine

400g canned Italian plum tomatoes

1 litre hot beef or chicken stock

2 bay leaves

sea salt and freshly ground black pepper

Cut the veal into medium cubes and coat generously with flour.

Heat 3 tablespoons olive oil in a heavy-based frying pan. Add the meat and brown for about 5 minutes, turning the veal pieces in the pan until well coloured on all sides.

Warm the remaining olive oil in a separate frying pan and sauté the onion, carrot and celery with the cloves over a medium heat until soft and golden. Add the meat and stir well for 3 minutes.

Pour in the wine and let the alcohol reduce and bubble away. Add the tomatoes, stock and bay leaves, and season with salt and pepper. Cook gently over a low heat for 2 hours, stirring occasionally. Remove the bay leaves and adjust the seasoning before serving.

TORTA DI CAPEZZANA
OLIVE OIL CAKE

SERVES 8

butter to grease tin

300g plain flour, plus extra to dust

1 tablespoon baking powder

3 large eggs

300g caster sugar

300ml finest extra-virgin olive oil

300ml milk

1 teaspoon grated orange zest

juice of 1 orange

Preheat the oven to 180°C/Gas 4. Butter and flour a 24cm cake tin. Sift together the flour and baking powder and set aside.

In a large bowl, beat the eggs and sugar together until pale yellow. Gently stir in the olive oil, milk, orange zest and juice, then add the flour mixture and stir just until blended.

Pour into the prepared cake tin and bake for about 45 minutes until the surface is golden brown and a fine skewer inserted into the centre comes out dry. Cool on a wire rack.

Paolo Fanciulli

'Pescaturismo'

'8:00am. Don't be late. The boat's called La Sirena – you can't miss her.' Paolo Fanciulli's voice is friendly and warm, but tinged with authority. Yes, he'll take us fishing with him. He'll even feed us breakfast and lunch. But if we're anything less than punctual, I have the feeling he'd leave us behind.

We find La Sirena easily enough, wedged between the sailboats and skiffs moored in the port of Talamone on the southern edge of what is said to be the last appreciable expanse of virgin coastland in all of Italy: *Il Parco Naturale dell'Uccellina*. We pile on board along with three other families (eight children and four languages between us), pick our way around a sprawling mound of fishing net (1½ kilometres unfurled), and take our places on low wooden benches lining the deck.

Most of the fisherman I've met have been taciturn bordering on gruff – shepherds of the sea, more at home mending nets than engaging in conversation. Not Paolo. Dressed in faded army fatigues, with cropped, sun-bleached hair and a sailor's tan, he's everywhere at once – asking our names; passing round newspaper clippings, photo albums and scientific journals; tying a motorised rubber dinghy up to the boat.

The sea is calm and shimmering blue, the day fair enough to see Monte Argentario and the island of Giglio on the horizon. As we set out of the harbour, Paolo's Austrian girlfriend Hildegard emerges from the cabin with breakfast: espresso, juice, *schiacciata* (salted flatbread) and an apricot tart. The lovely Hildegard is one of those unabashedly feminine women who make the rest of us feel like lumberjacks. Doe-eyed, pig-tailed and breathtakingly cleavaged, her voice bubbles out in a sing-song way as she cheerfully makes her way around the boat pouring coffee and pointing out landmarks.

Paolo wastes no time launching into the purpose for our excursion. We are
'pescaturisti' on board La Sirena, not only with the hope of hauling in something
delicious for lunch, but to learn the difference between sustainable fishing and the
ruinous fishing practices which have threatened the whole coastal eco-structure. He
doesn't address us formally as a group but speaks to each of us individually, thrusting
a newspaper article about net trawling into my hands while talking to a 9 year-old
French boy about 'fish houses' and endangered sea grasses. When I ask him how
long he's been a fisherman, he answers, *'da sempre'*. He's always been one, though
he didn't become an activist until 1986, at the age of 25.

'When I was a kid, the sea was full of fish.' He lowers his voice conspiratorially
to make his point and I find myself leaning forward to listen more intently. *'Ora il pesce
non c'è più.'* There are no fish anymore. Why? *'La pesca a strascico'* – commercial
trawlers dragging 5,000 kilo lead-weighted fishing nets along the coastal floor. 'They're
not allowed to fish in waters less than 50 metres deep or within 3 miles of the coast,
but they do it anyway.' The nets plough through everything in their path, decimating
plant life, breeding grounds and marine habitats. According to Paolo, for every kilo
of fish hauled in, the well-being of 100 kilos of sea life is compromised.

La Sirena rounds a rocky promontory and the village of Talamone disappears. We
coast along the edge of the park and its jagged crags dotted with dwarf palm trees,
swathes of green umbrella pines, stone watch towers and sandy coves. Its woods
are full of deer, wild boar, badgers and foxes; its trees with migratory birds. The park
would be a beautiful sight anywhere, but in Italy – where most of the coastline is
jammed with people, neon bright deck chairs, cabanas and restaurants – this level
of wilderness is astonishing.

Paolo tells us that the sea bed along the coast used to be as rich as the *macchia*
(wild Mediterranean scrubland) covering the park's hills. 'If people could see the coastal
floor the way they can see deforested woodlands, they would be outraged.' He gives
us an example: 'The sea grass *Posidonia oceanica* oxygenates the water, provides
a habitat for fish to lay their eggs, and prevents erosion of the coast.' He hands me
an underwater photograph of a *Posidonia* grassland hit by trawl nets. It has all the
desolation of an abandoned car park.

Two decades ago, Paolo decided to try to bring public and government awareness to the problems caused by trawl nets. He started by writing newspaper articles and appealing to government officials to come up with something more than the piddling 500 euro fine for trawlers caught violating the 3 mile/50 metre rule. By 1992 he came to the conclusion that bureaucratic channels would get him nowhere. 'That's when I came up with the *pescaturismo* idea,' he explains. It's a play on the popular *agriturismo* theme, where working farms let out rooms to travellers. 'People love this place. I figured that if I showed them what was going on, they'd spread the word and try to help.'

Paolo's ability to combine sobering reality with visionary optimism has served his cause well. For years he's helped champion the idea of planting what he calls '*case per i pesci*' (fish houses, otherwise prosaically known as 'dissuaders') along the coastal floor in places where trawl netting is prohibited. This summer almost 250 *dissuasori* (30 of which were paid for through contributions from Paolo and his *pescaturisti*) were finally installed along the Tuscan coast. They look a bit like enormous concrete bird houses, weigh a tonne and a half each, and are imbedded with hooks serious enough to tear right through a trawl net, if not bring down a boat. The idea is that the hooks keep the trawlers away, the hollow boxes become safe havens for fish to lay eggs, and the *Posidonia* returns to the sea bed to grow unmolested.

* * *

'We haven't seen a trawler since,' Paolo says elatedly. He pulls on a pair of electric orange rubber coveralls and elbow high gloves, then signals to his deckhand Marcus that he's ready to let out the net. For all its bulk, the net is a delicate, ephemeral thing, and as the boat moves forward in long, slow circles, Paolo guides it into the sea with his hands and it uncoils and blooms in the clear water. For a moment, he's no longer our guide, but a fisherman absorbed in his task. His work suit is as smooth as a seal's belly. As it is, a moment's distraction is all it takes to get caught in the net and dragged overboard to drown in a tangle of rope.

It is all well and good to see the net going into the water, but nothing compares to watching it come out. A pulley at the bow hoists it from the sea and on to the deck. '*Un grongo!*' Paolo pulls a conger eel from the net and tosses it into the icebox. '*Un pesce sorriso!*' A skate – too small to keep, though he has the kids run their fingers along its knobbly back before he throws it back into the sea. Paolo can tell what's in the net from 5 metres away: a grey mullet full of roe; a glimmering sea bream; a poisonous scorpion fish; a smooth bellied bonito. Seagulls hover waiting for cast offs: a half-eaten cuttlefish; a *pesce prete* who lost its eyes to a crab – the sea is rougher than its calm surface suggests. The kids are rapt and after 5 minutes they've forgotten their squeamishness and want to help. They untangle fish, throw back littles, whistle for seagulls and hound Paolo with questions. This is education as it is meant to be.

Net hauled in, deck swabbed, we are ferried by dingy to a deserted, pebbly beach on a driftwood strewn cove. Hildegard disappears into the woods with a pair of wicker hampers. Paolo sits at the edge of the shore, surrounded by the kids, gutting and scaling our catch. We adults mostly swim and laze in the sun.

'*Tutti a pranzo!*' Hildegard's voice rings out like a bell and we follow her up through the woods to a long wooden table and a simple outdoor kitchen tucked beneath a canopy of trees. There is Vermentino from the Maremma coastal valley – land of the supertuscans – chilled, crisp and so easy to drink that the first couple of glasses go down like water. 'We're going to have the pasta before the antipasti,' Paolo announces, 'because the flavour is *particolare*, and I want to make sure you really taste it.'

I peek at the saucepan over the stove. *Rossetti!* Tiny red fish – pale, pinky white when cooked, except for the black pinpoints of their eyes – second only to lobster in cost and even harder to come by. Hildegard's cooked them with shallots, wine and a hint of courgette, aubergine and capers. She tosses the pasta with the sauce, a grating of lemon zest and a sprinkling of parsley, then ladles it generously on to plates. She may not be Italian, but she cooks as if she were.

Next come *le bruschette semplici* (toasted bread with garlic and olive oil), covered in roasted red peppers, scattered with tomatoes and basil, and spooned over with the *rossetti* sauce. Paolo's also sliced the *palamita* (bonito) raw on to bread and drizzled it with olive oil. '*Sushi maremmano*,' he calls it. A wise person would pace himself throughout the meal, given the abundance of grilled fish we know awaits us. But we are not wise – we are happy, eating with abandon, senses warmed by the sun, the wine, the company and the deliciousness of everything we've tasted so far.

'Now you are going to see the difference between *pesce povero* and the real thing,' Paolo tells us. 'With fish this fresh, anything more than a squeeze of lemon, salt, olive oil and a few rosemary branches to brush the fish with is a crime.' When the platter arrives at the table, it is a revelation. '*Orata, dentice, mormora, sarago, mazzone, muggine...*' Paolo intones the names of the fish, and the sound is like an ode to a tired and beautiful sea.

PASTA ALLE ROSSETTI DI HILDEGARDE
HILDEGARDE'S PASTA WITH ROSSETTI

SERVES 4

4 tablespoons olive oil

1 small yellow onion, finely chopped

1 shallot, finely chopped

1 small aubergine, finely chopped

1 courgette, finely chopped

300g rossetti or any saltwater fish, filleted and cut into pieces or chunks

125ml dry white wine

1 dried chilli, crushed

1 teaspoon brine-cured capers, drained

400g penne or other dried pasta

sea salt

1 teaspoon grated lemon zest

1 tablespoon chopped flat-leaf parsley

Heat the olive oil in a frying pan and add the onion, shallot, aubergine and courgette. Sauté over a medium heat until the vegetables are soft, adding a bit of water to the pan if necessary.

Add the fish and cook over a medium-high heat for 3 minutes. Pour in the wine and simmer until the alcohol evaporates. Sprinkle in the chilli and capers and stir the sauce well.

Boil the pasta in abundant salted water. Stir the lemon zest and parsley into the sauce. Drain the pasta, toss well with the sauce and serve at once.

GRIGLIATA MISTA DI PESCE
MIXED GRILLED FISH

SERVES 6

3kg saltwater fish (bream, bass, red mullet and plaice are ideal), scaled and gutted

olive oil for brushing

4 branches of rosemary

sea salt and freshly ground black pepper

lemon wedges

Prepare a medium-hot charcoal grill or barbecue. Arrange the whole fish in an oiled, two-sided fish grilling rack. Fasten the rack so that the fish are held firmly inside.

Grill or barbecue until the skin is lightly browned and crisp, turning the rack once. Use the rosemary branches to brush the fish with olive oil as it cooks. Season with salt and pepper to taste and serve with lemon wedges.

POLENTA CON LE SEPPIE
POLENTA WITH CUTTLEFISH

SERVES 6

for the polenta
2 teaspoons salt
200g polenta

for the cuttlefish
1 kg small cuttlefish, with their ink sacs
5 tablespoons olive oil
1 yellow onion, finely chopped
2 garlic cloves, crushed
sea salt and freshly ground black pepper
125ml dry white wine

To make the polenta, bring 1.5 litres water to a gentle boil in a medium heavy-based saucepan. Add the salt. When the water returns to the boil, add the polenta in a fine, steady stream, stirring continuously with a wire whisk so that no lumps form. Reduce the heat to medium. After a few minutes, when the polenta begins to thicken, turn the heat right down.

Cook, stirring regularly with a wooden spoon, for 30–40 minutes. The polenta is ready when it comes away easily from the side of the pan.

To prepare the cuttlefish, pull the head and tentacles from the body pouch. Set aside the ink sacs and discard the transparent quill and other innards. Cut away the mouth and eyes. Rinse the pouch and tentacles under cold running water. Peel the grey membrane from the pouch. Roughly chop the tentacles and cut the pouches into 3cm rings or strips. Dilute the cuttlefish ink in a small glass of water and set aside.

Warm the olive oil in a frying pan. Add the onion and garlic and cook over a gentle heat until the onion is soft and transparent and the garlic golden. Add the cuttlefish and season with salt and pepper. Stir the cuttlefish in the pan for a moment, then pour in the wine and cook over a high heat until the alcohol has evaporated, no more than 2 minutes. Stir in the diluted cuttlefish ink and cook for another minute.

Ladle the polenta on to soup plates. Spoon the cuttlefish in its ink on top and serve.

CACCIUCCO
SEAFOOD STEW

SERVES 6

500g clams

salt

2.5kg assorted fish of different sizes, some whole (eg scorpion fish, gurnard, hake, bream, John Dory, grouper, grey mullet, monkfish)

500g large prawns in their shells

500g squid and/or cuttlefish

for the stock

1 yellow onion, peeled

1 carrot, peeled

1 celery stalk

handful of flat-leaf parsley

for the cacciucco

6 tablespoons olive oil

1 yellow onion, finely chopped

handful of flat-leaf parsley, chopped

4 garlic cloves, 3 crushed, 1 peeled

2 dried chillies, crushed

200ml dry red wine

800g canned Italian plum tomatoes, chopped

sea salt and freshly ground black pepper

6 slices country bread, toasted

To clean the clams, soak in plenty of cold salted water for 2 hours, changing the water several times. Scale, clean and fillet whole fish, reserving the heads and bones. Cut larger fillets into chunks. Rinse the prawns. Clean the squid/cuttlefish (see left) and cut into pieces, discarding the ink sacs.

To make the stock, pour 1.5 litres water into a stockpot and add the fish heads and bones, onion, carrot, celery and parsley. Bring to the boil, lower the heat and simmer for 40 minutes, skimming often. Discard the onion, celery and parsley, then pass the stock through a mouli (food mill) or press through a sieve. Return the stock to the pot and keep at a low simmer.

To make the cacciucco, heat the olive oil in a large cooking pot and add the chopped onion, parsley, crushed garlic and chillies. Sauté over a gentle heat until soft and fragrant, adding a bit of water to the pan if it dries out.

Add the squid and/or cuttlefish and stir well. Turn up the heat to high, pour in the wine and let bubble until the alcohol evaporates. Stir in the tomatoes and a generous ladleful of fish stock. Bring to the boil, then lower the heat and simmer for 15 minutes.

Add the fish fillets and pieces with two ladlefuls of stock and simmer for 15 minutes. Adjust the consistency if necessary by adding more stock; the soup should not be too dense. Season with salt and pepper to taste. Add the clams and prawns and simmer, covered, until the clam shells open and the prawns are pink.

Rub the toasted bread with the remaining garlic clove. Lay a slice of bread on the bottom of each soup plate. Ladle the cacciucco on top and serve.

Andrea Bertucci

Proprietor: *Osteria Il Vecchio Mulino*

You could spend your whole life in Tuscany and never get to the northwest edge of the region, known as the Garfagnana. Not that it isn't worth seeing. It's just the sort of place you're unlikely to happen upon by accident (few roads lead there, bordered as it is by the Apennines to the north and the Alpi Apuane to the west), and there's not much in the way of traditional attractions to get you there by design. Therein lies its loveliness.

The Garfagnana's high valleys are planted with golden fields of *farro* – an ancient grain, and the only one that grows happily there. Sleepy villages are scattered along the banks of the river Serchio and amidst forests of chestnut, oak and pine; lonely hamlets cling to steep hillsides. Shepherds tend goats, sheep and semi-wild pigs; cheese is made; meat is cured. An old watermill grinds corn, chestnuts and wheat into flour. There are wild berries in spring, mushrooms come autumn. In its isolation, simplicity and self-sufficiency, the Garfagnana evokes the memory of '*l'Italia di una volta*.' Its very ordinariness is its biggest charm.

If you speak to gastronomes about the food of the Garfagnana, they will invariably mention four things:

FARRO/EMMER WHEAT This grain is traditionally used in soups, but it is also wonderful in salads. Its production in the Garfagnana is protected by hard won IGP (*indicazione geografica protetta*) status. Farro (Triticum dicoccum)is not to be confused with its poor cousin, spelt (Triticum *spelta*).

FORMENTON OTTO FILE A rare maize, identifiable by its eight thick rows of red or golden kernels, and by the outstanding polenta it makes.

BIROLDO A local blood sausage made from the humblest bits of the pig. An impressive Slow Food Presidium product.

ANDREA BERTUCCI Cherubic-faced, much-beloved proprietor of the Osteria Vecchio Mulino – wine bar, eatery of sorts, specialty foods shop, and showcase for all things local and delectable.

* * *

One Saturday in August we drove through a lashing summer rain towards the town of Castelnuovo Garfagnana to have lunch at the Vecchio Mulino and see for ourselves what all the fuss was about. The road wound and climbed through the valley, tracing the liquid path of the Serchio. We parked at a crossroads, beside a wall of peeling billboards advertising a local beauty contest and an upcoming polenta

fete. Castelnuovo may well be considered the capital of the Garfagnana, but it felt like an intersection of roads leading from nowhere in particular to nowhere else.

Maybe it was the bleakness of the day and the weary air of the town that made the Osteria's first impression so potent, but as we rushed out of the rain and into the crowded room, my first sensation was that of being rescued. Andrea lifted his knife from an immense mortadella and waived us over to a table. The only other table in the room was already occupied by a handful of people sipping espressos amidst the detritus of what looks to have been a thoroughly enjoyed meal. Strains of a Puccini aria floated above voices in animated conversation.

We walked across the worn terrazzo floor, past a pale marble counter and its row of homely *torte* (one of which looked to be filled with greens, another with blueberries); past shelves laden with wine, sacks of polenta and *farro*, dried porcini mushrooms, speckled beans, jam (plum and redcurrant, but also persimmon, green tomato, leek and cardoon); and took our seats beside a great glass cabinet filled with local *formaggi* and *salumi*.

'*Ci penso io*?' You don't always want to hand over the pleasure of deciding what to eat when you're out – but in the right circumstances, it's foolish not to. '*Ci fidiamo*,' we answer. We trust. What followed was essentially a feast – despite its being made up of bite-size morsels brought to our table in a never-ending succession of round wooden chopping boards. '*Mangiate piano*,' Andrea admonished, setting down a bowl of crisp raw vegetables. '*Questo è slow food.*'

There were, among other things, dense little triangles of *torta salata* (three types: *farro*, potato and chard, the emphasis on dense); *affettati* (sliced meats) – the *biroldo* richly studded with meat and fat, the *prosciutto bazzone* deliciously reminiscent of Spanish *pata negra*; *insalata di farro* with tomato, cucumber, red onion and basil; and a selection of variously aged and sometimes rather barnyardy cheeses which we ate with potato bread and chestnut honey.

* * *

It's been 20 years since Andrea opened the Vecchio Mulino. 'At first I wanted to get rich quick,' he says with mock seriousness, 'but I ended up having much more fun tracking down the valley's farmers, shepherds, millers, cheesemakers… and bringing their things here.' Occasionally he has what he refers to as *assaggi culturali* (cultural tastings), inviting friends like Alvaro Ferrari, local organic *formenton otto file* grower to the Osteria to talk about and, of course, cook polenta.

Over the years the shop has evolved into a repository for the best the Garfagnana has to offer, so it seems paradoxical that Andrea's actually a bit vague about the exact provenance of his goodies. He seems, essentially, to be more a hunter-gatherer than the champion of any one, or group of, particular producers. When I asked him who made his savory *torte* he hesitated, then answered, '*la mia zia*' (my aunt). A few hours later I walked past a little deli near the church in Pieve Fosciana and there in the window were those very same tarts. '*Si, certo…* we make them for Andrea,' the baker informed me matter-of-factly.

I have the feeling Andrea told me what he thought I wanted to hear; that he believed it would make me happy to imagine his kind-hearted old auntie in her kitchen, flowered apron tied around her ample waist, rolling pin in her hand. I am happy imagining her… but the truth would have been just as nice.

INSALATA DI FARRO
FARRO SALAD

SERVES 4

150g pearled farro
sea salt and freshly ground black pepper
3 tomatoes, coarsely chopped
1 red onion, halved and thinly sliced
1 cucumber, peeled, halved lengthways
and sliced
2 handfuls of basil leaves
olive oil to drizzle

Put the farro in a medium saucepan with 1.5 litres water, salt lightly and bring to the boil. Reduce the heat to medium and simmer, partially covered, until the farro is tender but still firm, about 20 minutes. Drain well and tip into a bowl. Leave to cool.

Toss the cooled farro with the tomatoes, onion, cucumber and basil. Season to taste, dress with olive oil and serve at room temperature or chilled.

INFARINATA
CORNMEAL SOUP

SERVES 6

200g dried borlotti or cranberry beans, soaked
in cold water overnight
50g cured pork rind, coarsely chopped
3 tablespoons olive oil, plus extra to drizzle
50g pork lard
1 onion, finely chopped
1 carrot, finely chopped
1 celery stalk, finely chopped
1 garlic clove, finely chopped
1 rosemary sprig, finely chopped
500g cavalo nero or kale, sliced into strips,
ribs removed
2 potatoes, peeled and cut into chunks
1 tablespoon tomato purée
sea salt and freshly ground black pepper
300g coarse-grain polenta

Drain the beans and place in a saucepan with the pork rind and 2.5 litres water. Bring to the boil and simmer, partially covered, over a medium heat until the beans are soft and their skins are tender, about 1½ hours.

In another cooking pot, warm 3 tablespoons olive oil with the lard. Add the onion, carrot, celery, garlic and rosemary. Sauté over a medium heat, stirring frequently, until the vegetables are fragrant and have begun to soften.

Stir in the beans, together with their cooking water and the pork rind. Add the cabbage or kale, potatoes, tomato purée and seasoning. Simmer, partially covered, for 20 minutes.

Pour the polenta into the simmering soup in a thin stream, stirring continuously. Simmer gently for 40 minutes, stirring regularly and adding extra hot water if the soup becomes thicker than porridge. Taste and adjust the seasoning.

Ladle into soup bowls, drizzle with olive oil and serve immediately.

TORTA DI MIRTILLI
BLUEBERRY TART

SERVES 8

for the pastry

200g unsalted butter, at room temperature, plus extra to grease

90g granulated sugar

1 large egg, lightly beaten

250g plain white flour, plus extra to dust

pinch of salt

for the filling

1kg blueberries

200g caster sugar

1 tablespoon lemon juice

50g potato flour

To make the pastry, cream the butter and sugar together in a large bowl. Beat in the egg, then add the flour and salt and mix with a wooden spoon to form a rough dough.

Turn out on to a lightly floured work surface and knead very gently until smooth. Form the dough into a ball, wrap in cling film and refrigerate for a couple of hours.

For the filling, combine the blueberries, sugar and lemon juice in a bowl. Mix the potato flour to a paste with 3 tablespoons water, then stir into the filling. Crush the berries lightly with a wooden spoon and let the mixture stand for 20 minutes.

Preheat the oven to 180°C/Gas 4. Butter a 24cm straight-sided tart tin with a removable base. Roll out the pastry on a lightly floured surface to a circle, 2mm thick, and trim to a 24cm round, using the removable tin base as a guide. Keep the trimmings.

Lift the pastry on the rolling pin and drape it over the tart tin. Gently press into the base of the tin. Roll the pastry trimmings into a long rope, the thickness of a cigar, and lay it around the inside of the tin on the edge of the pastry. Press gently to connect the rope to the base of the tart and line the side of the tin, then use your thumb and forefinger to give the tart a fluted edge.

Prick the pastry base all over with a fork. Line the case with baking parchment and beans and bake blind for 20 minutes. Remove the paper and beans.

Pour the blueberry filling into the pastry case and bake until the crust is golden and the blueberries are bubbling, about 40 minutes. Place on a wire rack to cool. Serve warm or at room temperature.

Famiglia Tistarelli

Aia della Colonna Farm

The closest village to the 240 hectare Tistarelli farm is a speck on the map called Usi, off a tiny road on the way to nowhere. To reach it we take the coastal Aurelia highway south through what was once the most notoriously inhospitable terrain in Tuscany – a vast malarial swampland inhabited only by feral black horses, semi-wild cattle with curved white horns, and the legendary Maremman cowboys – *butteri* – who herded them. Under Mussolini, the flatlands were drained (which next to getting the trains running on time is his most oft-cited good work), and a system of irrigation channels devised which transformed the land into one of the most fertile agricultural areas in the region.

There seems to be no direct road to Usi so we aim for the Etruscan town of Scansano, turning away from the sea and continuing inland, just as the *butteri* once did during the transhumance, when they moved their herds to higher ground during the summers. It is slow going, but pleasantly so, the road meandering through a landscape of old oaks, vineyards, olive groves and stone farmhouses. Just past the sulphurous thermal springs of Saturnia we turn on to a narrow rutted road, which dips and climbs, until every bend seems to carry us further from civilisation.

On the windswept crest of a hill, with wide-open views of a countryside swathed in the bright greens of newly sprouted grains, we spot an old *casa colonica* (farmhouse) sharing its perch with a cement grey outbuilding in mid-construction. A hand-carved sign tells us we have arrived.

A little boy wearing a knitted woollen cap is running around the *aia* (the old threshing floor from which the farm takes its name), fighting an imaginary battle with a handmade wooden sword. His mother introduces herself as Roberta. We tell her we're looking for Roberto. 'That's my brother,' she says and volunteers the services of 3 year-old Lorenzo while we wait for his uncle to return from the fields.

'*Portali a vedere i maiali. Sú!*' Lorenzo races out of the courtyard, slashing the air with his sword and marching through every puddle in his path. He ignores the brood of small black turkeys scratching around in the dirt and leads us up a hill to a fenced acreage of well-trampled earth, housing a couple of dozen dusky grey pigs whose fore backs, middles and front legs are covered with a wide band of bristly white hair. They take one look at us and tear off on squat legs with an altogether un-porcine agility,

then turn back to stare at us from a safer distance. These are no ordinary barnyard swine lolling around in a pen fattening up on slop – they are *Cinta Senese*, indigenous to the countryside around Siena. Once a fixture on nearly every Tuscan farm, recently nearly extinct, they are currently the darlings of gastronomes who know a thing or two about the way Tuscan pork used to taste.

'Do you see how muscular they are?' asks Roberta. Muscular is not usually the first word that comes to mind when one thinks of pigs, but she's right. They do look like they've had their exercise. 'And look at their snouts.' All the better to forage with – the pigs spend a year in the *macchia* (Mediterranean woodland) where they scavenge for acorns, chestnuts, heather, roots, tubers and whatever else they can unearth with

their long, thin snouts. In winter, when foraging is scarce, they also feed on barley, field beans and oats grown and milled on the farm.

Tuscan farmers traditionally raised *Cinta Senese* because they could thrive unsheltered and find their own food in the woods. In the 50's, fast-growing foreign breeds were introduced that were considered more economical to farm, and the *Cinta* population – once over 20,000 sows – fell to less than 400. Only a few stubborn *contadini* ignored the trends and steadfastly held on to the old ways, the Tistarelli among them. In the last decade the breed has been rediscovered – to such fanfare that a *Cinta Senese* prosciutto or salame can now cost five or six times the price of one from an industrially farmed pig.

When Roberto shows up he has more than a few words to say about *Cinta*'s revival. 'It's not really fair to say you have a *Cinta* product just because it comes from a *Cinta* pig. How has that pig lived – in the wild or in a pen? What has it eaten? How has the meat been cured? If you treat it like a common farm-raised pig, it won't have the strong rich flavour of a *Cinta*.'

Aia della Colonna farm has managed to keep out of the worst of the commercial fray. Its animals – be they chickens, rabbits, turkeys, geese, lambs, *Cinta Senese* or Maremman cows (usually simply referred to as *maremmane* around here) – are largely reserved for family, friends, a few local restaurants and fortunate guests staying on the farm. 'We were the first *agriturismo* in the area,' says Roberta, referring to that marvellous Italian invention whereby working *fattorie* are licensed to let rooms to travellers and indulge them with farmhouse food and wine. Roberta, who is also a ceramicist, and her mother Livia run the *agriturismo* and its kitchen; Roberto and his father Geraldo tend the animals and pastures, and make *salumi* (cured meats) from the *Cinta Senese* pork.

For the past 11 years, the farm has been holistically organic – its semi-wild animals forage in untamed woods, its feed and grazing crops are organically grown, and its *salumi* produced without nitrates or preservatives. 'People thought we were crazy when we decided to go *biologico*,' says Roberto. 'No one could get their head around why we'd voluntarily choose to make the switch.'

We bid our goodbyes to the pigs and set off to see the *maremmane* and the horses Roberto uses to herd them. '*È un vero cowboy*,' says Roberta. '*Sapete*, he used to train horses for the *Palio*.' Pride in Maremma's *butteri* runs strong and deep. Stories abound about the time – more than a century ago – when local cowboys trounced Buffalo Bill in a riding contest. Over the years, the *buttero toscano* has assumed an almost mythical status in the collective consciousness. It's a compelling image: the solitary *cavaliere*, one hand on the reins of a muscular black horse, the other gripping the end of a long, hooked staff, moving a sea of long-horned cattle across a wild and desolate landscape.

Roberto refuses to be romanticised. 'You can't go near a *maremmana* on foot – you need either a horse or a tractor.' He loves horses – the choice was obvious. We approach a maze of tall wooden pens, all of them empty. 'The animals are only brought in to tag and check,' he explains, 'otherwise they live out in the woods and fields.' The farm's two massive bulls share a pasture with a pair of Maremman horses. The cows and their calves are in the bare winter woods – some stand and stare at us unblinking with liquid brown eyes, the others are stretched out under the trees, their lyre-shaped horns pale as birch bark. In this landscape they look mythical and primordial, but also somehow as if they belong.

* * *

We are invited back to the house for lunch – not in the *agriturismo* dining room, but at a wooden table in the old farmhouse kitchen. Geraldo is sitting on the wide lip of the hearth, poking at the embers around a pot of beans cooking by the fire. A cauldron of beef broth simmers on the stove. Lunch begins – as so many Tuscan meals do – with a platter of *affettati* (sliced cured meats), passed around the table by Roberto's girlfriend Veronica (a biologist who left northern Italy to come and work on the farm). The *Cinta Senese* prosciutto is less salty than common *prosciutto toscano*, but its flavour more earthy and wild; the *ammazzafegato* (a local salami known affectionately as the 'liver killer') spicy, pungent and vaguely offally; and the *capocollo* (a meaty salami) deliciously sweet, salty, spicy and peppery all at once.

Livia had decided this morning that we should have a *bollito* for lunch. 'There's no better way to try *maremmana* beef,' everyone agrees. 'You can't compare its flavour to any other beef,' says Livia. '*Maremmane* are essentially wild animals. Their meat is darker. Redder. A bit tough for a steak unless it's really well aged, but perfect for a *bollito* (boiled) or *stracotto* (slow-cooked roast).' First she ladles out the broth, into which she has whisked and simmered a mixture of beaten farmhouse eggs and grated parmesan. The meat is served sliced on a platter with homemade mayonnaise and *salsa verde*, the wine from homegrown grapes poured out of a ceramic carafe.

It's heartening to witness such joyful self-sufficiency in an age where tradition skills have so often been abandoned. 'I'd say Roberto's more attached to the *fattoria* than even I am,' says Girardo. 'The farm works because we do everything ourselves,' Livia explains. Roberta nods her head in agreement, but her brother concurs only up to a point. '*Funziona perché ci piace fare questa vita*!' It works because they like the life.

BOLLITO DI MANZO E VITELLONE
BOILED BEEF

SERVES 6

1kg beef (any combination of shoulder, brisket with some rib attached, silverside and tongue)
1 onion, peeled
1 carrot
1 celery stalk
1 ripe tomato
handful of flat-leaf parsley
handful of basil leaves
sea salt
pinch of black peppercorns

to serve
salsa verde
mayonnaise

Put all the ingredients in a large stockpot with 3 litres water. Bring to the boil, then reduce the heat to a simmer, and cook for 3 hours, skimming off the scum as it rises to the top from time to time.

Remove the meat from the pan (saving the stock to make a soup, see below). Peel away the skin from the tongue, carve the meat into slices and serve with salsa verde and mayonnaise.

STRACCIATELLA
BEEF BROTH WITH EGG & PARMESAN

SERVES 6

2 litres beef stock (see above)
4 tablespoons freshly grated parmesan
4 very fresh large eggs, well beaten
pinch of freshly grated nutmeg
freshly ground black pepper

Strain the meat and vegetables from the bollito and bring the stock to a simmer.

Beat the parmesan into the eggs and season with nutmeg and pepper. Pour the egg mixture into the stock and simmer for 5 minutes, stirring regularly. Ladle into soup bowls and serve.

MAIONESE
MAYONNAISE

MAKES 600ML

3 large egg yolks
2 tablespoons lemon juice
sea salt and freshly ground black pepper
600ml olive oil
1 teaspoon Dijon mustard

Put the egg yolks, lemon juice, a pinch of salt and a grinding of pepper in a bowl and whisk together until smooth. Slowly drizzle in the olive oil, drop by drop to begin with, then in a steady stream, while whisking continuously. Add only so much oil as can be absorbed by the egg mixture at one time.

Stir in the mustard, then check the seasoning. Serve at once, or refrigerate for up to 2 days.

SALSA VERDE
GREEN SAUCE

SERVES 6

1 garlic clove, peeled
1 salted anchovy, finely chopped
1 teaspoon brine-cured capers
large bunch of flat-leaf parsley, finely chopped
1 hard-boiled egg, finely chopped
4 tablespoons olive oil
sea salt and freshly ground black pepper

Pound the garlic, anchovy and capers, using a pestle and mortar. Stir in the parsley, chopped egg and olive oil, then season to taste with salt and pepper. Transfer to a serving bowl.

SFORMATO DI SPINACI

SPINACH FLAN

SERVES 6–8

for the béchamel sauce

50g butter

2 tablespoons plain flour

500ml milk

sea salt

pinch of freshly grated nutmeg

freshly ground white pepper

for the spinach

1.5kg spinach, washed

25g butter

30g parmesan, freshly grated

3 large eggs, separated

to assemble

25g butter, plus extra to grease tin

50g dried breadcrumbs

To make the béchamel sauce, melt the butter in a saucepan over a low heat. Add the flour and stir for 2–3 minutes until thickened, but not brown. Meanwhile, heat the milk in a separate pan to just below the boil. Slowly pour on to the roux mixture, whisking until smooth. Season with salt, nutmeg and white pepper to taste.

Cook over a low heat for about 3–4 minutes, stirring occasionally, until it forms a creamy sauce, thick enough to flow from a spoon. Remove from the heat and set aside to cool for 30 minutes or so.

Preheat the oven to 180°C/Gas 4. Cook the spinach briefly until tender in a pan over a medium heat with just the water clinging to the leaves after washing. Drain well. When cool enough to handle, squeeze out excess water and roughly chop.

Heat the butter in a frying pan. Add the spinach, season with salt and pepper and sauté until the spinach has lost all its liquid. Stir in the parmesan, egg yolks and 4 tablespoons of the béchamel.

In a clean, dry bowl, whisk the egg whites until stiff peaks form. Gently fold into the spinach mixture, using a metal spoon.

Butter a shallow baking tin (about 23 x 30cm) and dust with dried breadcrumbs. Spread the spinach mixture evenly in the tin and cover with the rest of the béchamel. Sprinkle with breadcrumbs and dot with butter.

Bake for 30 minutes, or until set and a light crust has formed on top. Serve warm, cut into squares.

Coltivatori di Carciofi di Chiusure

Half a dozen members of the newly formed *Associazione Il Castello di Chiusure* are gathered around a dining table at the Locanda Paradiso in the village of Chiusure (population of 90) on a Sunday afternoon in spring. The table is covered with a green and white checked cotton cloth, upon which sit a carafe of red wine, a bottle of olive oil (unlabelled, extra-virgin from the hills surrounding the village), and a collection of *carciofi di Chiusure* – small, smooth skinned, purple-leafed *morellini* artichokes – harvested earlier that morning from the vegetable gardens of those in attendance.

Lorenzo Lorenzini, active association member and author of a small book about his village's favourite edible, is at the head of the table. His leathery arms and damp, earth-smudged t-shirt give him the look of someone who spends more time in the *orto* (vegetable garden) than at a writing desk. He picks up a *carciofo* by its long rough stem, takes an imaginary drag on the unlit cigar between his teeth, and sets out to explain the whys and wherefores of the Chiusure artichoke. 'Look how purple the leaves are,' he says, proffering the *carciofo* as if he were presenting me with spring's first long-stemmed rose. 'Compare it to a commercial *morellino* grown in Maremma on the coast.' He reaches under the table and pulls one from a brown paper bag.

Now, it is true that Italians everywhere tend to believe that anything grown in their own backyard (actual or metaphorical) is better than the same thing coming from somewhere else. But it is also true that every so often the particular lay of the land, the texture of the soil, and the play between sun and wind and rain conspire to create a backyard particularly suited to the growing of a certain thing. Such is said to be the case with the artichokes of Chiusure.

We stare at the *carciofi* as if they were about to jump up from the table and begin singing their own praises. 'Squeeze them,' somebody says. A spongy artichoke is invariably a bitter, inedible thing. The Chiusure artichoke is firm and compact (the *morellino* from Maremma only slightly less so), its layers of concentric leaves packed tightly like the petals of an unopened flower. 'Rub the leaves together.' I do. They squeak. It seems that there's nothing exactly wrong with the Maremman artichoke, just that everything it is, the Chiusure artichoke is… and more.

'*È la terra*,' says Lorenzini, puffing once again on his unlit cigar. 'We're in the heartland of the Crete Senesi – the soil is a mixture of *creta* (mineral-rich clay) and *tufo* (porous rock). The mineral salts give our *carciofi* a richer colour, the clay in the soil retains moisture so well that the plants never need to be watered.'

I can't help but smile to hear Lorenzini describe the Crete Senesi so prosaically. The stone farmhouses, hill towns and cypresses of the countryside south of Siena – its sea of rolling hills, golden with grains in summer, tilled and dun in winter, a thousand shades of green in spring – have fed the fantasies of anyone who's ever dreamt of a Tuscan idyll. This is the landscape depicted in every calendar about Tuscany. This is the quintessential image of the place. And however cliché that image may have become, the place itself remains unutterably beautiful to behold.

* * *

'We began 3 years ago as a committee of local residents looking for ways to revitalise our village,' explains Ivano Scalabrelli, 64, a retired banker whose velvet waistcoat, knotted cravat and natty salt and pepper beard give him a vaguely theatrical, lord-of-the-manor air. 'This year we became an association. We already have 45 members – that's half the population of Chiusure.' He extracts an official-looking laminated membership card from his wallet and hands it to me for inspection.

'Artichokes have been cultivated in our hills since the Middle Ages. Monks grew them at Monte Oliveto Maggiore,' he explains, waiving an arm in the direction of the massive Benedictine monastery that sits across a steep, wooded ravine to the west of the village. 'Farmers grew them here.' After the end of World War II, Chiusure's population fell as farmers migrated to the cities looking for work. Fields went fallow, traditions wore thin. The village was on the way to becoming terminally sleepy – a charming, lifeless, 10-minute postcard-and-coffee-stop for tourists on their way to somewhere else.

And so the idea of reviving the cultivation of Chiusure's famed *carciofi* was born. As it was, nearly everyone with even a speck of land already had a vegetable garden. Chiusure is no different from the rest of Tuscany, or Italy for that matter, in its desire for fertile soil to be rendered productive rather than ornamental. Strange irony that Chiusure's unruly vegetable plots crowded with lettuces, onions, herbs, broad beans and artichokes are so much more beguiling than the average tidy front garden.

Renato Rosi, who has a fair sized *carciofaio* (artichoke plot) on the sloped edge of his garden, tells me that 3 years ago there were about 300 artichoke plants in Chiusure – perennials, producing about 10 artichokes each during spring. Today there are 1,000 of the silvery leafed plants, with plans to increase that number to 10,000. Earlier this month the Association's first gastronomic stand at the village fete was the main attraction.

'What's the best way to eat them?' I ask. Suddenly everyone is speaking at once. 'Fried,' suggests someone. '*Sì*, but that's a bad example – even shoe leathers taste good battered and fried,' retorts another. '*Crudi con pinzimonio*,' raw with seasoned olive oil, advocates someone else. 'Yes! They're good for the liver,' seconds another. Italians seem to have an acute awareness of the state of their vital organs in relation to everything they eat or drink. Only in Italy have I ever heard anyone say that eating something made their spleen hurt, or that a food was an *ammazzafegato* – a liver killer...

'The *pinzimonio*,' I ask, 'is it seasoned with salt, pepper and lemon juice?' Heads shake; tongues tsk. '*No. Sale, olio buono e basta.*' Just salt and good oil. There are collective murmurs of assent. When a Tuscan says *olio*, he means olive oil. And when he says *olio buono* he doesn't mean the most expensive bottle you can find, but oil from his own olives or the olives of someone he knows. We pour some *olio* into our own little glass pots, sprinkle in some salt and get down to the work of eating our artichokes. The conversation (more a free-for-all than a dialogue) continues as we pull off the leaves and dip them into the oil. It's like eating crisps only healthier.

I want to know how they preserve *carciofini*. 'Some people like to boil them in vinegar, others use white wine,' says Scalabrelli. 'For how long?' I ask. 'An hour.' '*Un'ora!*' cries Paradiso's owner Manuela Caselli, walking into the room with an artichoke omelette in one hand and a bowl of artichoke soup in the other. '*Perché*... how long do you cook them for?' '*Un minuto!*' Their laughter seems to acknowledge that in Italy there are always as many recipes as there are cooks, and that it is actually Scalabrelli's wife Fernanda who does the work of preserving at home. She appears a few minutes later with a fresh jar of *carciofini* under oil. Fernanda is of the camp that boils in vinegar – and her *carciofini* have a tarter edge than those boiled in wine. She is tactful about the boiling time issue, pausing and smiling at the group before resorting to that most common of all Italian culinary explanations: '*Li cucino quanto basta.*' She cooks them until they're ready.

A word about carciofi

However much you may like artichokes, it's hard to imagine them as a culinary sensation unless you've spent some time in Italy when they are in season. The artichokes of my American childhood were large and leathery, available year round, cooked one way only (boiled) and eaten with butter… end of story. In Italy, you can simply forget about artichokes when they aren't in season, except for those preserved in olive oil, which are truly delicious.

In their season – springtime, and in some places once again in the autumn – Tuscan *trattoria* menus abound with artichoke dishes. During the height of the season you can have a three-course meal with *carciofi* at every stage, and the best greengrocers might offer as many as four different types of artichokes for sale:

MAMME / LARGE ARTICHOKES   Familiar, weathered artichokes that are usually boiled. Sometimes they are stuffed.

CARCIOFI / SMALLER, SLENDER ARTICHOKES   Often sold with their long stems tied together in bunches, these have the same rough green leaves but (usually) no chokes. After cleaning down to their edible bits, they are sliced into wedges and used where needed – in pasta sauces, risottos, scattered over meat, for example. At the very least, they are eaten as a *contorno* (side dish) – boiled and dressed with olive oil and lemon; sautéed with garlic and parsley; or dipped in batter and deep-fried.

CARCIOFINI / TINY ARTICHOKES   The size of apricots, these are sold for canning. These are labour intensive – cleaning down to next to nothing – so it takes a lot to end up with any sort of quantity, but absolutely worth the effort.

MORELLINI / SMALL PURPLE-LEAFED ARTICHOKES   These are the prettiest of all and the only artichokes you'd ever want to eat raw (you'll be happy to do so when you've tried one). They are also wonderful cooked – as good as their rough green cousins. This is the variety grown in Chiusure (though most of the commercially grown *morellini* come from the Maremma on the southwest coast of Tuscany).

Cleaning artichokes

Fill a bowl with cold water and squeeze in the juice of a lemon. This will keep the artichokes from turning black once they've been cut. While you're at it, rub a little lemon juice on your fingers to keep them from staining.

Peel the outer leaves off each artichoke until you reach the tender yellow and purple tinged inner leaves. Turn each artichoke on its side and cut off the tough (sometimes spiked) leaf tips, so that only the tender, pale, edible part remains. Cut off all but 2–3cm of the stem and peel the retained part with a paring knife.

Slice the cleaned artichoke in half. Remove the hairy choke (if any) by running the tip of a small knife between the choke and the heart. All that remains is edible. Cut it into wedges or slices and soak in the lemony water until ready to use.

FRITTATA DI CARCIOFI
ARTICHOKE OMELETTE

SERVES 4

6 medium artichokes

juice of 1 lemon

2 tablespoons extra-virgin olive oil

25g butter

1 yellow onion, finely chopped

sea salt and freshly ground black pepper

8 very fresh large eggs

splash of milk

Clean the artichokes down to their hearts and edible leaves (see left), slice them into wedges and soak in water with the lemon juice added.

Heat the olive oil and butter in a medium frying pan (suitable for use under the grill) and sweat the chopped onion over a low heat until it begins to release its juices. Drain the artichoke pieces, pat dry, then add to the pan and season with salt and pepper. Increase the heat to medium and sauté until the artichokes are cooked but still firm.

Preheat the grill. Beat the eggs together with the milk and a pinch of salt.

Spread the artichokes evenly in the pan to form a single layer, then pour the eggs over them. Lower the heat slightly and cook slowly until the sides and bottom are set but the centre still loose (run a spatula around the edge every so often to keep the frittata from sticking).

Finish the omelette under the hot grill. It is ready when the centre has set and the surface is golden. Serve hot or warm, cut into wedges.

CARCIOFI SOTT'OLIO
BABY ARTICHOKES PRESERVED IN OLIVE OIL

MAKES ONE 500ML JAR

1kg smallest available artichokes

1 lemon, halved

1 teaspoon coarse sea salt

1 litre white table wine

1 teaspoon black peppercorns

about 500ml extra-virgin olive oil

Clean the artichokes down to their hearts and tender leaves (see left), but leave them whole. Rub the stem and cut edges with the lemon (rather than soak them in acidulated water).

Put the artichokes in a medium saucepan, add the salt, pour in the wine and bring to the boil. Lower the heat and simmer until the artichokes are cooked but still firm and the alcohol has evaporated. Lift them out of the pan with a slotted spoon and drain, stem side up, on a clean tea towel.

Spoon the artichokes into a sterilised preserving jar, scattering in the peppercorns as you do so. Cover completely with olive oil, then let the jar settle for a couple of hours to make sure no air pockets remain. Add more olive oil if necessary, close the jar tightly and store in a cool, dry place for 1 month before eating – they taste best when they've marinated a while.

CARCIOFI SALTATI CON AGLIO E PREZZEMOLO
SAUTEED ARTICHOKES WITH GARLIC & PARSLEY

SERVES 4

8 medium artichokes

juice of 1 lemon

4 tablespoons extra-virgin olive oil

3 garlic cloves, thinly sliced

splash of white wine

handful of flat-leaf parsley, chopped

sea salt and freshly ground black pepper

Clean the artichokes down to their edible parts (see page 120), slice into wedges and immerse in a bowl of water with the lemon juice added.

Warm the olive oil and garlic in a frying pan and cook over a low heat until the garlic is golden. Drain the artichokes, pat dry with kitchen paper and add to the pan. Sauté for a minute.

Turn up the heat, douse with white wine and cook until the alcohol evaporates. Sprinkle in the parsley, season with salt and pepper and continue cooking until the artichokes are tender, but still firm. Add a bit of water to the pan during cooking if it's getting too dry.

PINZIMONIO CON CARCIOFI
BABY ARTICHOKES WITH OLIVE OIL & SEA SALT

SERVES 4

8 very fresh baby artichokes

finest Tuscan extra-virgin olive oil

sea salt

Cut a fresh end on each artichoke stem and lay the artichokes on a platter in the centre of the table. Half-fill 4 ramekins with olive oil and sprinkle liberally with salt.

To eat, peel away the tough outer leaves of the artichoke until you arrive at the tender yellow inner leaves tinged with pink. Peel off a leaf at a time, hold it by its pointed tip and dip in the olive oil and salt. (There's no hairy choke to remove from artichokes this small and fresh.)

Cut the heart into halves or wedges and dip in the seasoned olive oil. The top 5cm of the peeled stems are delicious to eat as well.

Margherita and Francesca Padovani

Fonterenza Winemakers

Montalcino is the land of big wines: powerfully structured behemoths that live in the cellar for 5 years before seeing the light of day. Deep, ruby red and scented of everything from berries and spices to violets and tobacco, these are the sort of wines that need to breathe for hours before being poured into wide-bowled crystal, Bordeaux style glasses. *Vini* more likely to conjure up images of vast estates and fusty old aristocracy, than of Margherita and Francesca Padovani, 30 year-old twin sisters born and raised in Milan, Tuscans by choice rather than birth.

The handful of times I rang to see if Jason and I could visit the vineyard, Margherita always answered with the same polite response: 'Yes, of course.' (Rumble of a tractor in the background.) 'Just not this week... we're very busy right now.' When we finally made the journey, our timing couldn't have been worse.

We drove south of Montalcino, past the town of Sant'Angelo in Colle and turned down the rutted dirt road leading to Campi di Fonterenza, the old stone farmhouse Margherita and Francesca's parents bought just before the girls were born. Margherita answered the door with the phone in her hands and a stricken look on her face. '*Sta grandinando in vigna*.' Hail in the vineyard is a winemaker's worst nightmare – especially

just before harvest, when the grapes are full of juice and a passing hailstorm can do all the damage of a swarm of locusts in a wheat field. Some producers insure against it. Small growers can hardly bear the added expense. At the first flash of lightning, Francesca had headed out to the vineyard (a 10-minute drive). Margherita stayed home and waited for us.

We tiptoed into the house and sat down at a long wooden table in the kitchen to await Francesca's return. 'Shall I make us a coffee?' Margherita asked, fingering her long brown hair as if it were a string of rosary beads, then winding it into a bun and securing it with a pencil. The clock ticked. On the table sat a basket of late summer tomatoes beside a row of preserving jars waiting to be filled. A grey cat purred on the windowsill. We were quiet as church mice.

The crunch of wheels on gravel broke the silence. I felt like we were at a doctor's surgery waiting for a prognosis. '*Tutto ok*.' Francesca kicked off her muddy work boots and poured herself a coffee. 'How ok?' Margherita wanted to know. 'It came down

like little pebbles, but they melted the moment they hit anything.' She'd checked the vines. No harm done. 'You need to stay out of the vineyard,' Margherita said, a faint hint of a smile creeping on to her lips like the first sliver of a new moon. 'The last three times you've gone, it's rained.'

The twins have chosen what they call '*un approccio contadino*' (a farmer's approach) to winemaking. 'We're learning as we go along,' they explain. It's not as if they're newcomers to the land. Though they were educated in Milan, every summer holiday, long weekend and Christmas break was an excuse to head down to Montalcino. Their family didn't grow wine grapes, but they pressed olives from their trees for oil, and the rhythms of the countryside became their own. Strange irony that the 400 year-old farmhouse's cellar and wine room had been converted into the girls' bedroom and playroom when they were children – only to be restored to their original purpose by the girls as adults.

Margherita went to university in Milan in 1997 to study literature. She barely lasted out the year. 'It wasn't for me. I went straight to Fonterenza, got a job in an *agriturismo*, and planted 2 acres of Sangiovese on a piece of land my mother had owned for years.' She tilled the soil and pulled up everything but two huge old oak trees. You don't usually see a sprawling *quercia* in the middle of a vineyard. 'I'm not in this *per fare business*. I love this place and this life. Those trees needed to stay.'

Francesca joined Margherita in 2000 after a stint in Scotland and some time on her own. 'We balance each other,' she says. Margherita likes making wine more than selling it. Francesca relishes getting their wine out into the world… and proving naysayers wrong. 'People thought we were crazy – two young sisters in Montalcino trying to make Brunello all on their own. Nobody thought we could do it.'

When they speak of making wine 'on their own,' they mean it in the most literal sense. They are the antithesis of gentlewomen farmers who dabble in viticulture without actually getting their hands dirty. If there's a tractor in the vineyard, one of them is driving it. When it's pruning time, they both work their way methodically up and down the rows of vines. 'Our goal is to be completely independent,' says Margherita. 'We've always had a few guardian angels help out during the harvest, but otherwise, we have no employees. It's just us.'

The vineyard has grown to 4.2 hectares – all but 5,000 square metres of which is planted with Sangiovese. The half-hectare of Cabernet Sauvignon Francesca chalks down to inexperience. 'We had prepared the land for planting, but there was no Sangiovese stock to be found anywhere.' Luckily, the resulting wine, Lupo di Fonterenza (100% Cabernet, named after a beloved dog), has turned out to be a pleasure, both in the making and in the glass.

Fonterenza adheres to biodynamic standards, both in the vineyard and the cellar. Biodynamics takes a holistic approach to organic farming, following the rhythm of the seasons, weather, sun and moon, and paying close attention to the interrelation of every aspect of farming – from water management to soil fertility and pest control. Rather than resorting to synthetic fertilisers, fungicides and pesticides to combat disease in the vineyard, the winery uses only copper, sulphur and plant extracts like willow, yarrow, horsetail, camomile and nettle. Camomile tea (sprayed rather than

sipped), has the same stress-relieving effect on plants as it does on humans; nettles work against aphids. The land is fertilised with manure from organically certified cattle breeders and by sowing leguminous plants after the harvest and ploughing them into the soil in spring.

We walk around the womb shaped *Vigna del Bosco*, its name inspired by the fact that the gently sloping plot of land is enveloped in native woodland. The grapes hang low on the vine and are so deeply coloured that to our untrained eyes, they look ready for picking. 'When will you harvest?' Jason asks. '*Buona domanda*. Not yet. They're still too high in alcohol, too acidic, and the seeds aren't mature enough.'

Everything would depend on the weather. The girls wanted to try to keep the grapes on the vine as long as possible. In a perfect world, there would be a couple more weeks of sunshine, but slightly cooler temperatures. A bit of rain would be good, but not too much or sugar levels would decrease and there'd be the risk of mould. One year the girls lost their bet with the weather and with it, 50% of their grapes.

In any event, the harvest is unlikely to be done in one go. Anyone who thinks that the task is pure manual labour hasn't been with Margherita and Francesca during *la vendemmia*. Last year they combed the vines eight separate times, picking only the very ripest grapes and eliminating any that didn't make the grade. Nonetheless, yields in the vineyard are intentionally low – 40 quintals per hectare – much lower than those permitted by DOCG regulations. 'We don't want the bunches touching each other when they're mature so we do a green harvest in late spring,' Francesca explains, referring to the practice of pruning away a portion of immature grapes to induce the vines to put all their energy into the remaining bunches.

* * *

When we return to Fonterenza a month later, we find Margherita much relaxed and dressed in jeans, a wine stained t-shirt and green rubber boots. She is four rungs up a metal ladder, pushing a cap of grape skins down into a vat of fermenting red wine, a traditional vinification practice known as *la follatura*. Francesca was in Rome hand delivering a shipment of wine, though when I'd spoken to her the day before she had been in the vineyard sowing field beans.

The harvest was all in and it was good. 'This year the grapes were really healthy.' Today Margherita is all smiles. 'It took twelve of us 3 days to bring them all in.' They had just received the latest alcohol analysis: 14.5%. She opens the spigot of a conical wooden fermentation vat, pours a few centimetres of brilliantly purple newborn wine into a tasting glass and holds it under her nose. 'Yesterday it smelled like cauliflower,' she says, happy as if she'd told us it smelled of roses. 'When you make wine naturally, it is so alive. It reacts to everything. One day it tastes of one thing; the next day of something else.'

Margherita tells me that this year Brunello di Montalcino, Rosso di Montalcino (a younger, fresher version of Brunello), a *vin rosato* (rosé) and Lupo di Fonterenza Cabernet will be produced under the Fonterenza label. But when I try to get her to give me a portrait of Fonterenza wines, she tells me she cannot. 'Our wines are the fruit of what's happened in the vineyard. They have a personality. They tell an ever-changing story… about the grape, the earth, our labour. Each year our wine will tell you that story.'

RISOTTO AL MIDOLLO DI BUE
RISOTTO WITH MARROW

SERVES 6

for the stock

1kg beef chuck or brisket

1kg veal marrow bones, each about 10cm long

½ stewing chicken (boiling fowl)

1 onion (unpeeled)

2 carrots

2 celery stalks

1 ripe tomato

2 bay leaves

sea salt and freshly ground black pepper

for the risotto

75g butter

1 onion, finely chopped

450g arborio or carnaroli rice

500ml red wine

100g parmesan, freshly grated

For the stock, put all the ingredients into a large cooking pot with 3 litres cold water. Bring to the boil and skim off any scum from the surface. Reduce the heat to low and simmer, partially covered, for 3 hours. Adjust the seasoning and skim any fat off the surface.

Strain the stock through a colander into a clean pan. Save the marrow bones.

For the risotto, keep the stock simmering gently in a pan on the back of the hob. Melt half the butter in a large heavy-based saucepan. Add the onion and cook over a low heat until soft and translucent, adding a little stock to the pan now and then to keep it from browning.

Increase the heat to medium and add the rice, stirring with a wooden spoon for a couple of minutes to coat the grains with butter and lightly toast them. Pour in the wine and let bubble until the alcohol has evaporated.

Ladle in enough stock to barely cover the rice and cook, stirring, until the liquid is absorbed. Continue adding stock in small amounts as each addition is absorbed, stirring almost continuously. When the rice has been cooking for 15 minutes, spoon the marrow from the bones and stir it into the rice. Add another ladleful of stock and cook until it is absorbed, stirring regularly.

When the rice is creamy and tender but still firm to the bite (about 18 minutes in total), remove from the heat and stir in the remaining butter and grated parmesan. Taste and adjust the seasoning.

Let the risotto rest for a couple of minutes, then spoon into individual serving bowls.

COSCIOTTO D'AGNELLO
ARROSTO

ROAST LEG OF LAMB

SERVES 6

1 leg of lamb, about 2.5kg
5 garlic cloves, roughly chopped
4 rosemary sprigs, roughly broken
sea salt and freshly ground black pepper
60ml white wine
4 tablespoons olive oil
handful of ripe cherry tomatoes, halved

Cut 4 long slits in the meaty part of the lamb and fill with garlic and rosemary. Season the lamb well and place in a suitable container. Whisk together the wine and olive oil and pour over the meat. Cover and leave to marinate in the fridge for at least 5 hours, overnight if you like.

Preheat the oven to 200°C/Gas 6. Lay the leg, meaty side up, in a roasting pan and roast for 1½ hours, or longer for well done meat. When almost cooked, remove from the oven and rub the cut tomato halves over the meat. Return to the oven for 10 minutes. Rest the meat for 10 minutes before carving.

FINOCCHIO AL BURRO
E PARMIGIANO

BRAISED FENNEL WITH PARMESAN

SERVES 4

4 fennel bulbs, trimmed
5 tablespoons olive oil
sea salt and freshly ground black pepper
50g parmesan, freshly grated

Peel the tough outer layer from each fennel bulb, then cut into medium wedges.

Warm the olive oil in a saucepan. Add the fennel and sauté briefly until it begins to wilt and release its juices, then add a few tablespoons of water and season with salt and plenty of pepper. Cover and cook for about 15 minutes until the fennel is soft but not mushy, stirring occasionally and adding extra water as necessary to prevent sticking.

Stir in the grated parmesan and grind over some more black pepper to serve.

MARMELLATA
DI CIPOLLA

ONION MARMALADE

MAKES ABOUT 500G

1kg sweet onions, such as Tropea, Vidalia or Maui
100g salt
5cm cinnamon stick
½ teaspoon cumin seeds
4 cloves
1kg caster sugar
600ml balsamic vinegar
200ml cider vinegar

Halve and thinly slice the onions and place in a bowl. Add the salt, toss well and leave to stand for 5 hours, to allow the onions to release their liquid. Rinse the onions under cold running water and pat dry.

Tie the spices up in a square of muslin and place in a medium saucepan with the sugar and both vinegars. Bring the mixture to the boil, stirring regularly until the sugar dissolves.

Add the onions and bring back to a simmer. Cook until the onions are transparent and the liquid is dark and syrupy, about 1 hour. Refrigerate when cool. Serve with boiled or roasted meats.

Silvano Mugnaini

Mushroom Hunter

It took me 15 years to convince Silvano Mugnaini to take me mushroom hunting with him. Back in the days when he was my gardener, I'd wake up some mornings to find a wicker basket filled with porcini mushrooms on my doorstep. They were always perfect specimens, fit for a botanical illustration or a book of fairy tales: smooth, pinky brown caps; firm underbellies; bulbous white stems (without a trace of worminess); and they smelled deliciously of the forest floor.

Silvano's generosity, it must be said, only extended as far as the mushrooms themselves. When I'd ask where his hunting grounds were, he'd look down at his muddy work boots and mumble, '*nel bosco*.' In the woods. When I wondered whether I could come along on an expedition, he answered that it was the sort of thing he liked to do *da solo*. Alone.

Those baskets of mushrooms thrilled and alarmed me in equal measure. Thrilled, because they were, after all, porcini – and I'm as enamoured with their musky earthiness as everyone else is around here. Alarmed, because I'd be relying entirely on my gardener's hand-on-his-heart assurances that eating them would not kill me.

There is no shortage of places in Tuscany where you can take foraged mushrooms to be identified and declared harmless and edible. But people like Silvano rarely use

them. Dyed-in-the-wool *fungaioli* are quite certain they know what may go into their baskets and what must stay in the woods. Mostly they are right. I trusted that Silvano knew the difference between an *amanita falloide* (fatally toxic, no antidote) and a porcino. I just couldn't stop thinking about those headlines that appear punctually in the newspapers when the weather turns warm and damp: 'Mushroom Hunter Hospitalised with Liver Failure...'

Ultimately my hunger always won out over what I concluded were irrational fears, stemming from the lack of foraging in my own gastronomic history. In the end, I'd cook the mushrooms, but I never entirely conquered the sensation of holding my breath when we lifted our forks.

* * *

Jason and my lesson in mushroom hunting began before we even left the house. We were to meet Silvano the second Monday in September. I rang him on the Sunday night. 'We can go for a walk... but we won't find anything,' he said. 'It's still too hot!' There'd been a bit of rain, but not enough. 'Besides,' he added, 'It's windy. *Funghi* are like fog – a little wind and *phfft*, they're gone.'

Two days later the weather broke and the sky came down in heavy grey sheets of rain. When the storm was over, the temperature had fallen, but the air felt close and sticky. Silvano phoned. 'This is good. *La terra ribolle*.' The earth is boiling over. Fermenting. That's exactly what it felt like. According to Silvano, the rain couldn't have come at a better time: a fortnight before the new moon. We agreed to meet in 3 weeks.

I rang the night before to confirm. For the past week, Silvano had been finding more mushrooms than he could legally take home in a day (there's a 3 kilo limit). 'We have to get started early,' he said. 'Too many people around once the sun is up. You don't want them to see where you're looking.' We were further instructed to bring a mushroom hunting permit, our old Jeep and a wicker basket. The first (which we could procure at the post office), because we weren't residents in the Casentino valley where we'd be hunting; the second, because the sturdier the car, the more distance

we could put between ourselves and other mushroom hunters; and the last, because the forestry service fines anyone they catch carrying mushrooms in a plastic bag. Spores fall through the holes in woven baskets while mushroomers amble about. Walking through the right sort of woods with a *cestino* of porcini is as good as casting seeds in the garden.

* * *

We met Silvano at a café halfway up the steep road leading to the *Passo della Consuma* and the high valleys and forests of the Casentino. There were wooden crates of mushrooms for sale and trays of salted flatbread studded with porcini. We bought three pieces of bread and had them wrapped in waxed paper for our *merenda* (elevenses).

When we turned off the main road, the landscape opened up into wide green pastures, rolling hills and woodlands. Silvano held forth from the back seat, his voice at full volume, barely drawing breath. 'It is a waste of time to run all over creation looking for mushrooms. Choose your area and stick to it.' Now that he had decided to bring us along, he seemed intent on telling us every trick of the trade. 'You must pay attention

to the weather in your hunting grounds – follow the temperature, rainfall, wind, humidity. *Tutti i giorni.*' Every single day.

It didn't take long to figure out why we'd been asked to bring the Jeep. The car had been put through its paces during the 10 years I owned it, but it had never seen roads like these. Rutted is an understatement. So is muddy. But just when it seemed like our old beast had accomplished the impossible, we'd pass yet another battered Fiat Panda parked on the side of the road, its owner already deep in the woods searching for *funghi.*

Silvano had us hide the car in a pine grove on a bed of dry needles. '*Zitti*!' he said in a hushed voice. 'No speaking unless absolutely necessary. If I need your attention I'll tap my sticks together.' Mushroom hunters always carry a staff to poke around trees and lift up leaves (in case there's a snake instead of a mushroom hiding underneath). Silvano carried two. We followed him into a chestnut and oak wood – the porcino's favourite habitat.

The ground was covered in the warm, muted colours of autumn – leaves in shades of yellow, orange and brown; bristly green scrub. Silvano seemed to be walking quickly for someone who was supposed to be looking for something, tapping the ground with his staffs in a way that reminded me of a blind person with a walking stick. 'You can feel with your staff when there's a mushroom hiding somewhere,' he whispered. 'And if you see a little bulge in the leaves, there might be a *fungo* underneath.'

Jason found a stick of his own; I scoured the ground for bulges; Silvano zigzagged through the woods. Tap… tap… tap, tap, tap, tap! '*Venite, venite*!' Silvano's excited whisper sounded more like a hiss. We squatted on our haunches around a tiny mound at the base of a chestnut tree. Silvano lifted off the leaves with tip of his wooden stick. '*Ecco*!' He sounded relieved. It wouldn't do to go home with an empty basket.

The *fungo* was lovely – a perfectly formed porcino – not huge, but big enough. 'Sometimes when it's warm, and there's no wind, and the moon is right, I'd leave a mushroom like this – cover it up and come back the next day. It could double in size overnight.' Not today. He eased the porcino out of the ground with his staff and brushed the soil off its knobby end.

Jason found the next mushroom in the same grove. 'I knew you'd find one!' Silvano shouted, the noisemaking ban temporarily lifted. Jason was delighted, but he swiftly fell from grace. '*Giù le mani*!' Silvano bellowed when he caught Jason pushing aside leaves willy-nilly, in search of more mushrooms. 'Stop! You can't bulldoze!' A day-old porcino is the size of a pin head. One careless swipe will yank it out of the ground.

Suitably humbled we trailed after Silvano like faithful hounds. He pointed out the occasional poisonous mushroom (which always looked innocuous enough) and unearthed a few more porcini. I don't think I'd ever have found one myself had Silvano not practically led me to it by the hand. Even then, when it was right under my nose, it took a minute before I could actually see its pale brown cap hidden among the scattered humus, leaves and twigs. I carefully pulled it from the ground. It smelled like autumn… and later tasted just as sweet.

TAGLIOLINI AI FINFERLI
TAGLIOLINI WITH CHANTERELLES

SERVES 4–6

1kg chanterelle mushrooms

25g butter

2 tablespoons olive oil

1 white onion, finely chopped

1 teaspoon thyme leaves

sea salt and freshly ground black pepper

125ml dry white wine

75ml double cream

500g tagliolini (or linguini)

freshly grated parmesan to serve

Clean the mushrooms with a soft cloth or mushroom brush, then cut into medium slices.

Heat the butter and olive oil in a pan and sweat the onion over a low heat until it is soft and translucent. Increase the heat to medium. Add the mushrooms and thyme, season with salt and pepper, and sauté for a couple of minutes.

Pour in the wine, let bubble until the alcohol has evaporated, then stir in the cream. Simmer over a gentle heat for a minute to let the sauce thicken.

Boil the pasta in abundant salted water until tender but slightly undercooked. Drain, reserving a little of the cooking water.

Toss the tagliolini briefly with the sauce over a low heat, adding some of the reserved cooking water if the pasta seems too dry. Offer grated parmesan at the table.

CAPPELLE DI PORCINI ALLA GRIGLIA
GRILLED PORCINI MUSHROOM CAPS

Remove the stem from a fresh, firm porcini mushroom whose cap is at least as large as your palm. (One cap is enough per person.) Wipe the mushroom clean with a damp cloth or mushroom brush. Make several incisions throughout the cap and fill with slivers of garlic and a sprinkling of salt. Brush the cap with olive oil and cook under a medium-hot grill, or barbecue, on both sides until soft and browned. Eat alone or atop a grilled steak.

ZUPPA DI PORCINI E PATATE
PORCINI & POTATO SOUP

SERVES 4

750g floury potatoes, peeled
3 tablespoons olive oil
2 medium yellow onions, finely chopped
1 litre hot chicken stock
sea salt and freshly ground black pepper
½ recipe porcini trifolati (see right)

Cut the potatoes into small chunks and set aside.
Put the olive oil and onions in a cooking pot over a
low heat and cook, stirring frequently, until the
onions are soft and fragrant. Add the potatoes and
sauté until they colour slightly, stirring regularly to
keep them from sticking to the pan.

Add the chicken stock and season with salt and
pepper to taste. Simmer, partially covered, until the
potatoes begin to disintegrate. Purée the soup
with a hand-held stick blender; or whisk briskly
using a hand whisk. Stir in the sautéed
mushrooms, simmer for 5 minutes and serve.

PORCINI TRIFOLATI

PORCINI MUSHROOMS WITH GARLIC & WILD MINT

SERVES 4–6

1kg porcini mushrooms

80ml olive oil

3 garlic cloves, thinly sliced

75ml dry white wine

2 tablespoons calamint (nepitella) or chopped flat-leaf parsley

sea salt and freshly ground black pepper

Wipe the porcini clean with a damp cloth or kitchen paper. Separate the stems from the caps if the mushrooms are large, and cut each into thick slices. Smaller porcini can be sliced whole.

Heat the olive oil and garlic in a heavy-based frying pan over a medium heat until the garlic is golden but not brown. Add the porcini and stir with a wooden spoon until they begin to wilt. Pour in the wine and stir until the alcohol evaporates.

Sprinkle with the calamint or parsley and season with salt and pepper. Reduce the heat to low and sauté gently for a further 15 minutes, stirring often.

Famiglia Busatti Sassolini

Artisan Linens

Morning light blazes across the high Tiber valley – source of the river that flows down to Rome – into a room whose windows are draped in fine ivory linen. There is a table covered with damask cloth and embroidered napkins, white on white, ironed to crisp perfection. A cupboard holds neat stacks of tea towels – linen, cotton, striped, flowery, some in pale earth tones, others in the bright colours of spring. There are hand towels cut from the same heavy cloth, their edges carefully crocheted, cross-stitched or fringed with tassels. The muted thrum of what sounds like a dozen printing presses drifts up through the floorboards. This is not a house, but a shop. Those are not printing presses, but looms.

Elena Busatti Sassolini greets me with a smile. 'My brother Giovanni will be here in a minute. He'll show you around the mill. I need to stay and mind the store.' I wander around the shop trying to imagine the *corredo* (trousseau) that would have been mine if I'd been lucky enough to have been born Italian.

My reveries are interrupted by the arrival of Giovanni who introduces himself as Nanni, takes me by the arm and guides me up the stairs to a study jammed with family portraits, photographs and leather bound books. Something about him is immediately

likeable. He wears his 61 years honestly, but there is a boyish twinkle in his eye and a sort of straightforward friendliness to his manner that puts me instantly at ease. He launches into the history of the Busatti family mill – a story that unfolds over seven generations in the hill town of Anghiari on the eastern edge of Tuscany.

'Giovanni, Francesca, Livio, Giuseppe, Mario, Giovanni Battista, Niccolò,' Nanni runs through the family tree, starting with himself and counting back through the generations on his fingers until he is satisfied that he's left no one out. The Busatti family history is tied to the Napoleonic invasions of the 18th century. In the second half of the 1700's, Niccolò Busatti opened a bakery in Anghiari. The venture was so successful that some years later his son opened a general store on the site where the Busatti mill and linen shop now stand. The store offered a bit of everything – bread, cured meat, yarn – it even lent money. When Napoleon's troops arrived, they took over the place and converted it into a woollen mill to make uniforms for the French army. The Busattis retired to the countryside to farm and wait out the occupation. When some 17 years later Anghiari was returned to Tuscany, the site was given to the family as war reparations by the Grand Duke and Gianni's great uncle Mario converted it into a full fledged mill.

* * *

Alongside the family portraits is a framed yellowed paper that looks like some primitive form of handwritten sheet music, all horizontal lines and scattered dots. Written along the top are the words, '*coperta bella a rosa. Isolina.*' Nanni explains that the lines and dots are actually weaving instructions for a pretty rose blanket, and that Isolina would have been a local woman who wove for the Busattis from home. 'Farming families never wanted to send their women outside the house to work. We supplied small looms all over the valley and bought back the fabric. We still do.' In fact, every morning a handful of people show up at the mill to pick up thread to weave into cloth, tablecloths to embroider, towels to hemstitch, and whatever else needs the skilful attention of able hands. Twice a year everyone convenes at the Busatti country house where the local priest says mass and more than 50 people sit down to lunch at one long table.

Nanni is intent on showing me two more portraits before we visit the mill. '*Ecco nonno Livio,*' he says. 'My grandfather was an amazing man... a catholic socialist. I have never known anyone else who so resolutely followed his principles. At the end of every year he would tally up his family's living expenses and donate that same amount to charity.' Nanni moves on to a photograph of his parents, a handsome couple surrounded by eight children (of which he was the youngest of six boys). 'My father died when I was 14 years old. *Nonno* Livio had passed away the year before. After that, everything changed.'

By everything he seems to mean a certain ease of life. His mother didn't have the first idea how to run the business. She gave her children education and culture, showered them with love and hoped that somehow providence would provide. It did... up to a point. Nanni left Italy in his 20's to travel the world selling tractors. 'I spent

showered them with love and hoped that somehow providence would provide. It did… up to a point. Nanni left Italy in his 20's to travel the world selling tractors. 'I spent time in America, in Africa, the Middle East… it was fantastic.' But in the end, he missed home. 'I missed these crazy old looms that break down every 3 minutes and still manage to produce such beautiful fabrics. These days I get homesick if I go more than a week without seeing a row of cypresses or an old stone church.'

* * *

We descend two flights of stairs into the bowels of the *palazzo*, the clatter of shuttles getting louder with every step. There are the looms, covered with lint, surprisingly delicate machines made of wood and iron. Each marches to its own tune of warp and weft – *ordito e trama* – the warp threads tight as the strings of a harp, the weft threads spinning off the bobbins, shuttled endlessly back and forth, the patterns revealing themselves excruciatingly slowly, one meticulous row at a time.

The whole of Tuscan history seems to be woven into the bolts of cloth. 'The stripes are the colours of the *arti fiorentine*: red for butchers (better to hide bloodstains), blue for bakers, yellow for goldsmiths and green for greengrocers.' We move to the oldest loom (vintage 1878, the others are from the 1930's), which is weaving a spray of pale green olive branches with linen threads. 'This is a 15th century pattern – things like olive branches, grapevines, cardoons and sprigs of wheat are all old traditional designs.' He moves to another loom. 'The two stags looking at the tree of life is from a Lorenzetti painting in the Duomo of Siena.' Another cloth is bordered with a pale blue frieze inspired from a glazed terracotta Luca Della Robbia bas-relief.

Nanni picks up a length of cloth, holds it under his nose and inhales deeply. 'You can still smell the vinegar we use to fix the colours.' The Busatti mill still dyes its best wool and linen with natural colours they extract themselves. 'The blue comes from *guado* (dyer's woad) – poor man's indigo; the yellowish green from broom flowers and leaves. We dye the yarn and thread right outside the mill and dry it on rush mats, just like they did hundreds of years ago. It's completely non-polluting so we can do it right here in the centre of town.'

In another room, wool is being spun into yarn. 'We buy sheared wool from shepherds all over the valley.' He opens a burlap sack and hands me a wad of *lana* fresh off the sheep, still studded with burrs and bits of grass, redolent of animal and lanolin. Ancient cast-iron machines beat the wool clean, wash, oil (with olive oil of course) and card it before it is spun. 'We make woollen robes for the monks of Camaldoli (the 11th century monastery in the Casentino forest north of Anghiari).' At this point I am hardly surprised to learn that the Vatican commissioned the Busattis to weave simple white cotton veils bordered with blue stripes as a gift for Mother Theresa of Calcutta.

What I am left wondering is whether there will be an eighth generation of Busattis to carry on the family trade. 'At first I thought not. My eldest studied at Stanford in America and now works designing helicopters. He couldn't be less interested in the mill. Livio, my second, is studying law. But Stefano, my youngest… I have hope. He's just out of high school and full of ideas. We fight about how things are done at the mill… but they're the right kind of arguments. He's interested. The seed's been planted.'

SPAGHETTI AL SUGO FINTO
SPAGHETTI WITH 'FAKE SAUCE'

SERVES 6

50g pork lard, chopped
4 tablespoons olive oil
1 large red onion, finely chopped
2 celery stalks, finely chopped
handful of flat-leaf parsley, finely chopped
500g ripe tomatoes, peeled, deseeded and coarsely chopped
12 basil leaves, torn
sea salt and freshly ground black pepper
500g spaghetti
freshly grated parmesan to serve

Heat the lard and olive oil in a medium, heavy-based saucepan over a low heat. Add the onion, celery and chopped parsley and sauté gently until the vegetables have softened but not browned.

Add the tomatoes with the basil and season with salt and pepper. Simmer for 15 minutes, stirring regularly. Check the seasoning.

Cook the spaghetti in plenty of boiling salted water until al dente. Drain, then toss with the sauce. Hand round grated parmesan at the table.

CONIGLIO AI CAPPERI
RABBIT WITH CAPERS

SERVES 4

4 tablespoons olive oil
4 garlic cloves, crushed
1 rabbit, about 1.5kg, cut into 8 pieces
4 tablespoons brine-cured capers, drained
4 ripe tomatoes, peeled, deseeded and coarsely chopped
sea salt and freshly ground black pepper

Heat the olive oil and garlic in a large heavy-based frying pan over a medium heat until the garlic is golden, then add the rabbit pieces and brown on all sides.

Add the capers and tomatoes, then lower the heat and cook for about 1 hour, occasionally stirring and turning the rabbit pieces. Halfway through cooking, season to taste with salt and pepper.

When most of the pan juices have been absorbed, add 120ml water and stir well. Continue cooking until the meat has soaked up most of the liquid and the rabbit is tender when prodded with a fork.

PATATE ARROSTO ALLE ERBE
HERBED ROASTED POTATOES

SERVES 4–6

4 garlic cloves, peeled
2 rosemary sprigs (leaves only)
6 sage leaves
1 thyme sprig (leaves only)
sea salt and freshly ground black pepper
1kg new potatoes
5 tablespoons olive oil

Preheat the oven to 200°C/Gas 6.

Chop the garlic and herb leaves together as finely as possible. Season with salt and pepper.

Peel the potatoes, cut into chunks and place in a roasting pan. Sprinkle with the herb mixture. Pour the olive oil over the potatoes, then toss to coat with the herbs, oil and seasoning.

Roast in the oven for about 1 hour until the potatoes are golden and cooked through, turning them over in the pan occasionally so that they brown evenly and don't stick.

TORTA DI MELE
APPLE TORTE

SERVES 8

butter to grease tin
150g plain flour (unbleached)
1 tablespoon baking powder
2 medium eggs
½ teaspoon vanilla extract
100g caster sugar, plus 1 tablespoon
250ml whole milk
100g unsalted butter, plus 1 tablespoon, melted
5 large or 6 medium cooking apples

Preheat the oven to 180°C/Gas 4. Butter a 28cm tart tin. Sift the flour with the baking powder.

Beat the eggs, vanilla extract and 1 tablespoon sugar together in a bowl. Slowly add the flour, milk and 1 tablespoon melted butter, stirring constantly until the mixture is smooth. Pour into the prepared tart tin.

Peel, core and slice the apples. Scatter them over the cake mixture and gently press down until they are either coated with the mixture or submerged.

Pour the 100g melted butter over the top and sprinkle with the 100g sugar. Bake for 40 minutes or until the surface of the torte is golden. Serve warm or at room temperature.

Giovanni Fabbri

Artisan Pasta Maker

'Did you know that San Lorenzo is the patron saint of pasta makers?' asks Giovanni Fabbri, pulling a lever on a hulking green pasta machine. After some rumbling and groaning, the machine dutifully begins pushing ribbons of *pappardelle di San Lorenzo* out of its yawning mouth. The edges are straight on one side and ruffled on the other. The straw yellow pasta takes its name from the patron saint's feast day in renaissance Florence, an occasion when *pastai* in the city's San Lorenzo quarter decorated their shops with the long pale noodles and the church broke them up into broth to offer to the poor.

'Most pastas get their names from the thing they look like,' Giovanni explains, his booming baritone voice more reminiscent of an old time radio announcer's than a fourth generation pasta maker's. *Ave Marie* (Hail Mary's) and *Pater Nostri* (Our Father's) are named after the beads on a rosary. There are *semi di mela* (apple seeds) and *fior d'olivo* (olive blossoms); *lumache piccole* (little snails) and *lumaconi* (big ones); *creste di gallo* (rooster's crests) and *cavatappi* (corkscrews); *capelli d'angelo* (angel's hair) and *occhi di ladro* (thieves' eyes).

We walk into a small room beside the pasta machine where rows of heavy bronze *trafile* (dies) patterned with the designs for scores of pasta shapes are stored. 'This is the *patrimonio* of the *pastificio*,' Giovanni says proudly. Some of the dies are as old as the place itself, which was first opened as a bakery, *pastificio* and grocery store by his great, great grandfather in 1893.

* * *

The main square of a small rural town in the heart of Tuscan wine country seems a strange place for a pasta factory, even an artisan one. Giovanni disagrees. 'A hundred years ago the countryside around here was covered in wheat fields,' he explains. Over the last 50 years, olives and wine grapes have mostly replaced *grano* and redefined the local landscape and economy, though the *pastificio* still buys Tuscan wheat grown around Siena, Grosseto and Pisa.

A lot has changed since the days when Fabbri spaghetti was air-dried on racks right in the square, bought by weight and carried home wrapped in brown paper and tucked under one arm, like a baguette. The recipe remains unaltered – nothing more than semolina and water – though with the arrival of electricity in the early 1900's,

the Fabbri's horse and millstones were retired. From then on, the dough was worked by machine and the pasta slow dried in heated cupboards inside the *pastificio*.

* * *

Before we talk about the differences between dried *pasta artigianale* and the industrially produced stuff, Giovanni wants to address the distinction between fresh pasta (think ravioli, tortellini and little old grandmothers with rolling pins) and dried pasta made from durum wheat semolina. 'One isn't better than the other,' he's quick to explain. 'They're simply two different things.' Fresh pasta is happy in lasagne, ravioli or bathed in a creamy sauce. Dried pasta is toothy – strong enough to hold up to the quintessentially Tuscan flavours and textures of things like beans, game meats and pecorino cheese. Fresh pasta likes butter. Dried pasta loves olive oil.

'*Ti faccio vedere*,' says Giovanni, making two little piles of wheat berries on the table, then taking one from each and biting into it. The first, *grano tenero* (from which fresh pasta is made) is the dusky yellow of dried corn on the outside, but floury white inside. The second grain, *grano duro* (durum wheat which is ground into *semola*) is hard, brittle and uniformly yellow throughout. *Grano tenero* is milled into soft white flour – but its glutens aren't strong enough to make a pasta that won't break, so eggs are added to help bind the dough and give it elasticity. Semolina is grittier than flour – full of gluten, and so difficult to work by hand that it is traditionally pressed through bronze dies, then cut and slowly dried.

If the difference between fresh and dried pasta is obvious, the one between artisan and industrially made dried pasta is huge. 'Two things make our pasta better than the industrially manufactured variety,' says Giovanni: 'Its texture and the temperature at which it is produced.'

'*Senti. È ruvido*', he says, opening the door of a drying cupboard and running his fingers through the long strands of spaghetti looped over metal rods to dry. The pasta looks smooth but is in fact slightly rough to the touch – a result of the dough's slow movement through the bronze dies. This texture enables the pasta to hold its sauce better than smooth, slippery industrially made pasta.

Giovanni is even more adamant about the importance of production temperature. 'We want to conserve everything that nature has given us in the grain,' he explains. If at any time during its production, the temperature exceeds 38°C, the glutens are altered, and the pasta's ability to absorb water and sauce is compromised. Pasta that's made commercially is dried in as little as 10 hours. Pasta Fabbri takes anywhere from 2 to 5 days to dry.

* * *

I leave the *pastificio* that afternoon with an armload of pasta and the recipe for *Nastroni sulla 'Nana'*, Giovanni's mother-in-law's famous pasta with duck sauce, which she always makes with the family's own ducks in celebration of *la battitura* – the threshing of the wheat. When I ask Giovanni for a recipe for the sort of pasta he'd be happy to eat any day of the week, he doesn't hesitate. '*Pasta al dente con un filo d'olio. Tutto lì*.' Boiled, but not overly so, and drizzled with olive oil. That's all.

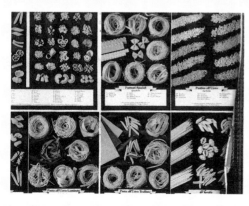

SPAGHETTONI CON CACIO E PIZZICO
SPAGHETTI WITH AGED PECORINO & BLACK PEPPER

SERVES 4

400g dried spaghettoni or thick spaghetti

sea salt and freshly ground black pepper

4 tablespoons olive oil

100g aged pecorino (ewe's milk) cheese, grated or crumbled

Add the spaghetti to a large pan of boiling salted water and cook until al dente. Drain, reserving a ladleful of the cooking liquid.

Toss the pasta with the olive oil and pecorino, and season generously with black pepper. If the pasta is a bit dry, add some of the reserved cooking liquid and toss well. Serve at once.

PENNE ALLA FIESOLANA
PENNE WITH PROSCIUTTO, CREAM & PARMESAN

SERVES 4

20g butter

1 tablespoon plain flour

250ml milk, heated but not boiling

sea salt and freshly ground black pepper

80ml cream

3 tablespoons freshly grated parmesan, plus extra to serve

2 tablespoons olive oil

70g thickly sliced prosciutto, cut into small dice

400g dried penne

2 tablespoons finely chopped flat-leaf parsley

Warm the butter in a small saucepan. Stir in the flour and cook, stirring continuously until the mixture smells faintly of biscuits; do not brown. Slowly whisk in the warm milk, season with salt and pepper and cook until the mixture thickens into a thin sauce. Remove from the heat and stir in the cream and parmesan.

Heat the olive oil in a small frying pan and gently sauté the prosciutto until lightly coloured. Remove from the heat and stir in the cream sauce.

Cook the penne in abundant salted water until al dente. Drain and toss with the sauce. Ladle into individual serving bowls and sprinkle with parsley. Offer grated parmesan at the table.

NASTRONI SULLA 'NANA'
PASTA RIBBONS WITH DUCK SAUCE

SERVES 6

4 tablespoons olive oil
1 onion, finely chopped
1 carrot, finely chopped
1 celery stalk, finely chopped
1 small duck, cleaned and cut into 8 pieces
100g thickly sliced prosciutto, chopped
handful of flat-leaf parsley, chopped
handful of basil leaves, torn into pieces
60ml white wine
800g tomatoes, peeled, deseeded and chopped
sea salt and freshly ground black pepper
500g dried wide pasta noodles (such as pappardelle)

Warm the olive oil in a large frying pan. Add the onion, carrot and celery and cook over a medium heat until soft. Lay the duck pieces in the pan, then add the prosciutto, parsley and basil. Cook, turning the duck, until lightly browned on both sides.

Pour in the wine and let the alcohol evaporate, then add the tomatoes and season with salt and pepper. Cook over a low heat for 30 minutes, adding a little water if the pan begins to dry out.

Remove from the heat and lift out the duck on to a board. Pass the sauce through a mouli (hand mill) or mash with a fork. Remove the skin and bones from the duck, slice the flesh and return to the pan with the sauce. Check the seasoning.

Bring a large pan of water to the boil. Add salt and return to the boil. Cook the pasta until al dente. Drain, toss with the sauce and serve immediately.

Walter Tripodi

Chef di Cucina: La Frateria di Padre Eligio

The blue and white ceramic sign marking the entrance to the *Frateria di Padre Eligio* reads '*Pace e Bene* (Peace and All Good), Comunità Mondo X Cetona.' It is dusk, later than we intended to arrive at the restored Franciscan monastery in the southern hills of Tuscany, and the place is bathed in silence. Not an unearthly one, but a sort of peaceful quiet that that makes us instinctively speak in hushed voices. '*Salve. Buona Sera.*' Jason and I are greeted by a lanky 20 year-old, wearing a black jacket over a crisp white shirt. He leads us through a cloister up to our bedroom – one of the seven open to the *Frateria's* paying guests.

The doorway is low and we bow our heads to enter the room. The bed is properly generous (not two singles pushed together) and made up with hand-embroidered linen sheets. A polished wooden writing desk sits at one end of the room; windows open on to immaculately tended gardens; there is no television; no internet access; no telephone.

We haven't actually come for the pure, unfettered luxury of the rooms, but for a place at the *Frateria's* table and a rumoured-to-be transcendent seven-course meal prepared by Walter Tripodi, its extraordinary head chef.

Walter Tripodi was 24 years old when he arrived at the *Frateria di Padre Eligio* in the *Convento di San Francesco* with few skills and the determination to kick a bad habit. The 13th century convent had become home to a group of recovering drug addicts working and living under the auspices of Mondo X, an outreach program founded by the Franciscan monk Padre Eligio. 'I was unhappy with my life. I wanted to change, but I knew I couldn't do it on my own. So I came here.' That was more than 20 years ago. He's never left. It's not that he's incapable of living in the 'real' world outside the confines of the *Frateria* and the thirty some Mondo X communities throughout Italy. It's that he doesn't want to. He's found a level of purpose and meaning in his work at the *Frateria* that would be next to impossible to replicate in a traditional restaurant kitchen.

* * *

We freshen up and make our way through a labyrinth of corridors and courtyards to an intimate dining room where two other couples are engrossed in the procession of delights appearing on their tables. Simone, our waiter, pours us sparkling

wine and brings out a platter of prosciutto and salami, a basket of assorted bread rolls and two pâtés – one of black olives, the other of capers – to dip them in. 'We make all our own *salumi* (cured meats), the wine and olives come from our community up the road, and the capers from the island of Formica off the coast of Trapini in Sicily where we have another community,' he tells us.

Between them, the Mondo X communities are 90% self-sufficient for their food needs. Their economy seems to function virtually autonomously. No one pays – or is paid – to live or work at a Mondo X community and there is no state funding for any of their projects or expenses. They have around 1,200 olive trees, 8 hectares of vegetable garden and an acre of vineyard. They raise farm animals – cows, pigs, rabbits, turkeys, chickens and guinea fowl. The bread in our basket was baked in the convent's 500 year-old wood burning oven.

Our meal went on for hours. The *salumi* were followed by a radicchio salad scattered with green beans, tomatoes and moist pieces of guinea fowl, which had been baked in parchment with herbs. Next came a pale yellow risotto with saffron, swordfish and mussels; then ravioli filled with ricotta and wild nettles in a buttery sauce flavoured with caramelised garlic; followed by rich, dark pigeon, split and cooked with sweet Vin Santo, raisins and pine nuts. Simone managed to be attentive and solicitous without a trace of the cloying waiterly affectation that can ruin an excellent meal. We were dipping into citrus sorbet and dark chocolate *biscotti*, when Walter arrived at our table wearing chef's whites and a gentle smile. '*Riposatevi bene... ci vediamo domani mattina.*' Rest well... see you in the morning.

* * *

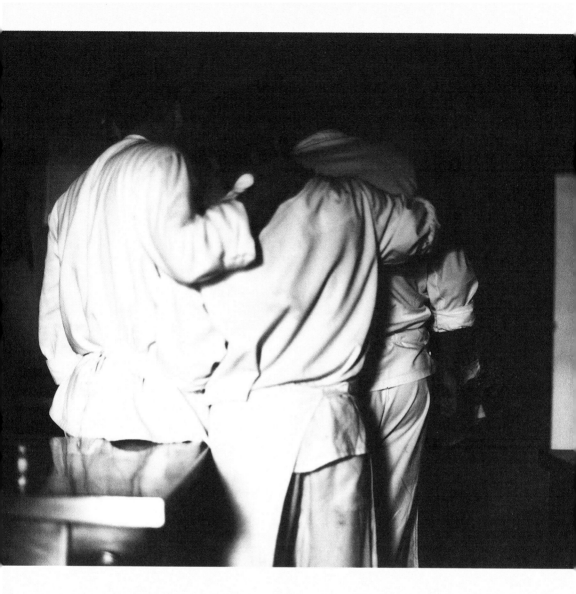

The community convenes every morning in the chapel at 6:30am for matins. Their voices drifted into the garden, lovely and heartfelt. We met Walter after breakfast in the cloister outside the kitchen. By now, the *ragazzi* (kids, as Padre Eligio calls them, though they range from as young as 14 to middle age) have set off for work – in the kitchen, tending the garden, clearing the woods, forging iron, sculpting travertine, working wood, embroidering – doing whatever it is that needs to be done.

The evidence of their labours is everywhere – at the table, of course, but also in a vegetable garden that looks like something out of a fairy tale; in masses of roses that spill over stone walls; in a delicate iron gate opening into a cloister; and in impossibly thin travertine bowls that look at once ancient and contemporary. Everything seems imbued with beauty and grace. 'The *Convento* was derelict in 1979,' says Walter. 'The community restored it over 18 years.' He hands me a calendar in which each month juxtaposes photographs of the convent before and after restoration. The transformation is astonishing. It looks much more as if it were the work of master artisans than of a bunch of kids trying to get themselves out of trouble.

'There is a structure to our days of work and study, but only one fixed rule – that no one be left alone,' Walter explains. 'When kids arrive here they aren't lucid or balanced. At the beginning we employed psychologists and doctors but found that didn't really help. What a young person in crisis needs is to rediscover himself – through a life of dignity, of values and clarity. That is what is offered here.' His words carry the weight of his own experience.

Walter takes pains to make sure we understand what the community is and what it isn't. 'This is not a religious community, even though there are signs of the church everywhere.' No one is required to attend mass, though in practice almost everyone does. 'It is not a rehabilitation centre but a *comunità di vita*.' A community of life. *Tempora tempera tempore* (time tempers us) are the watchwords of Mondo X; the rooster, the first animal to awake on the farm, its symbol. 'No one is in charge here. Padre Eligio comes and goes. The transformation from someone who has chosen death to someone who chooses life comes through dialogue, discussion, introspection, respect for others, care of oneself, and the quality of attention brought to ones work.'

Sometimes a passion is borne of that work. It was Padre Eligio who suggested that Walter try working in the kitchen. 'I started like everyone does – washing dishes, baking bread, cooking for the community – moving up the ranks until I had my turn at the cooker. Over the years I've had three real teachers,' he says, 'Gerard Boyer, from Reims in France taught me how to organise a kitchen; Cesare Giaccone, who has been called one of the world's best Italian chefs, taught me to really understand my raw ingredients; and Mario Buffone, one of the founders of Mondo X, taught me about effort, sacrifice and constancy. Three different schools… but each taught me something important.'

* * *

A bell sounds and the *ragazzi* begin to file into the refectory for lunch. '*Ciao, Chef*,' they say to Walter as they pass. The tables are set in a U so that everyone can see each other. A wood carving offers a simple prayer of blessing, humility and gratitude. 'Meals are when we come together as a community. To talk about what's happening in the world, deal with any problems that have come up, and just be in each other's company.' The last person in closes the door behind her. 'Their privacy is sacred,' Walter says to us. We are not invited in.

'Do you ever go on holiday?' I wonder. He looks at me as if the thought had never occurred to him. 'I go to visit my family in Calabria, but otherwise, no. My life is here. I find it fascinating and fulfilling. I've never made the decision to stay here forever – it's a conscious choice to live my life this way that I renew every year.'

INSALATA DI FARAONA CON RADICCHIO E FINOCCHIO

SALAD OF GUINEA FOWL, RADICCHIO & FENNEL

SERVES 6

for the guinea fowl

1 oven-ready guinea fowl
2 rosemary sprigs (leaves only)
2 sage sprigs (leaves only)
10 juniper berries
3 garlic cloves, sliced
sea salt and freshly ground black pepper

for the salad

generous handful of green beans
2 ripe tomatoes
2 fennel bulbs
olive oil to drizzle
lemon juice to drizzle
3 small heads of radicchio, washed

for the dressing

8 tablespoons olive oil
juice of 1 lemon
splash of white wine vinegar
2 teaspoons salted capers, rinsed

Preheat the oven to 180°C/Gas 4. Rinse the guinea fowl under cold running water and pat dry. Combine the herbs, juniper berries and garlic in a bowl and season generously. Rub half the mixture inside the guinea fowl and scatter the rest on top.

Wrap the guinea fowl in baking parchment, folding in the sides to seal well and securing with kitchen string if necessary. Bake for 1½ hours.

In the meantime, prepare the salad. Boil the green beans in salted water for 3 minutes, then drain and plunge them into cold water. Drain and pat dry.

Immerse the tomatoes in a bowl of boiling water for a minute. Remove and peel away their skins, then halve, deseed and roughly chop the flesh.

Slice the fennel as thinly as possible and arrange on salad plates to cover the base. Drizzle with olive oil and lemon juice, sprinkle with salt and set aside.

When the guinea fowl is cooked, take out of the parchment and place on a board. Once cool enough to handle, remove the skin and shred the meat. Whisk the dressing ingredients together to combine. Toss the meat in the dressing.

Peel the radicchio, leaf by leaf, and arrange in a layer on top of the fennel on each salad plate. Scatter the chopped tomatoes, shredded meat and green beans over the top and serve.

RAVIOLI CON LE ORTICHE AL BURRO E AGLIO
NETTLE & RICOTTA RAVIOLI IN GARLIC BUTTER

SERVES 6

for the filling
200g ewe's milk ricotta cheese
500g tender nettle leaves (or spinach or Swiss chard)
60g parmesan, freshly grated
1 egg yolk
pinch of ground cinnamon
pinch of freshly grated nutmeg
sea salt and freshly ground black pepper

for the pasta
400g '00' pasta flour, plus extra to dust
pinch of sea salt
4 large eggs
1 tablespoon extra-virgin olive oil

for the sauce
6 garlic cloves, peeled
75ml white wine vinegar
90g butter
1 tablespoon sugar
freshly ground white pepper

to serve
few thyme sprigs
freshly grated parmesan

For the filling, put the ricotta in a muslin-lined colander and leave to drain.

If using nettles, wear rubber gloves when handling them raw. Cut the stems and ribs from the greens, then wash the leaves in several changes of cold water. Drain in a colander. Cook until tender, with the water clinging to their leaves after washing (adding a bit more to the pan if necessary). Drain and let cool, then form into a ball and squeeze out as much water as possible. Finely chop the leaves and squeeze again.

Put the chopped greens in a bowl with the ricotta and the parmesan, egg yolk and spices. Mix with a wooden spoon to a smooth paste, then season with salt and pepper to taste. Set aside.

To make the pasta, pile the flour into a mound on a clean surface and make a well in the centre. Sprinkle with the salt. Break the eggs into the well,

add the olive oil and beat lightly with a fork. Use one hand to swirl the egg mix in a circular motion so that the flour is gradually drawn in from the sides of the well. When the mixture forms a rough dough, use both hands to incorporate enough of the remaining flour to make a dough that is tacky, but doesn't stick to your hands. Clean the surface, and wash and dry your hands.

Dust your surface lightly with flour and knead the dough for about 8 minutes until it is smooth and elastic, adding extra flour in small increments if it is sticking to your hands. Roll out the dough by hand or machine. If rolling by hand, first wrap the dough tightly in cling film and set aside to rest – anywhere from 20 minutes to 3 hours.

To roll out by machine, divide the dough into 6 balls and cover with a damp tea towel. Set the machine rollers on the widest setting. Flatten a ball into a rectangle with your hands and feed it through the rollers. (Lightly dust with flour if sticky). Fold the dough into thirds and pass through the rollers again. Repeat 3 or 4 times until the dough is soft and pliant. Adjust the setting to bring the rollers one notch closer. Run the dough strip through the rollers twice without folding. Continue bringing the rollers together one notch at a time and feeding the dough through until it has been through twice at the second finest setting. Lay the dough strip on a floured surface and repeat with the remaining dough balls.

To roll out by hand, divide the dough into 3 pieces. Place one on a floured surface, flatten slightly and use a rolling pin to gently roll out the dough, starting at the centre of the ball and rolling outwards, rotating and turning the dough over so that it rolls out evenly and as thinly as possible.

Using a straight-edged pastry wheel, cut the dough into long strips, 7–8cm wide. Spoon heaped teaspoonfuls of filling along the bottom third of the pasta strips at 4cm intervals. Brush water around each dollop of filling, then gently fold the strip over to enclose the filling. Seal around each mound of filling, gently pressing out any air

with your fingertips. Use a straight-edged or fluted pastry wheel to cut 4cm squares. Repeat with the remaining pasta strips and filling.

To make the sauce, put the garlic in a small bowl, cover with salt and leave to stand for 1 hour. Rinse and pat dry, then add the garlic to a small pan of cold water and bring to the boil. Remove the garlic, refill the pan with fresh cold water and repeat. Once again, repeat the process, this time adding 1 tablespoon of the vinegar to the water. Drain the garlic and pat dry.

Melt the butter in a small frying pan. Add the garlic and sugar and cook until the sugar dissolves. Add the remaining 60ml wine vinegar, season with salt and white pepper and cook until the garlic is lightly caramelised (blonde rather than brown).

To cook the ravioli, bring a large pot of water to the boil. Add salt and return to the boil, then add the ravioli. Cook until al dente, about 3 minutes. Drain and divide among warm bowls. Spoon over the sauce and garnish with thyme and a sprinkling of grated parmesan. Serve at once.

PICCIONE CON PINOLI E UVETTA
BRAISED PIGEON WITH PINE NUTS & RAISINS

SERVES 4

2 pigeons, cleaned

2 tablespoons red wine vinegar

6 tablespoons olive oil

about 100ml Vin Santo

1 yellow onion, finely chopped

1 celery stalk, diced

1 garlic clove, crushed

1 bay leaf

2 tablespoons raisins

2 tablespoons pine nuts, toasted

Preheat the oven to 160°C/Gas 3. Split the pigeons in half, removing the breastbone, so you have 4 portions, each with one boned breast attached to the thigh and leg.

Place the pigeons in a bowl. Pour over the wine vinegar, 3 tablespoons olive oil and 2 tablespoons Vin Santo. Set aside to marinate for 15 minutes, then drain.

Warm 3 tablespoons olive oil in a flameproof casserole. Add the onion, celery, garlic and bay leaf and sauté over a low heat for a few minutes.

Lay the pigeon halves in the casserole, add a splash of Vin Santo and 75ml water, then cover and braise in the oven for 1½ hours. Meanwhile, soak the raisins in warm water to cover for 20 minutes, then drain.

Lift the pigeon halves on to a warm platter. Pour the pan juices into a small bowl and whisk in 4 tablespoons Vin Santo. Add the raisins and pine nuts, spoon over the pigeon and serve.

BISCOTTI AL CIOCCOLATO
CHOCOLATE BISCOTTI

MAKES ABOUT 24

200g butter, softened, plus extra to grease

200g plain, dark chocolate

125g caster sugar

125g soft brown sugar

250g plain flour, plus extra for dusting

2 large eggs, lightly beaten

Preheat the oven to 180°C/Gas 4. Lightly butter a 23 x 33cm shallow baking tin. Using a sharp knife or a vegetable peeler, pare the chocolate into thin shavings; set aside.

Put the butter, sugars, flour and eggs in a separate bowl and mix thoroughly to a smooth dough. Stir in the chocolate shavings. Use a spatula to spread the dough evenly in the prepared tin and bake for 20 minutes.

Remove from the oven and reduce the oven setting to 100°C/Gas ¼. Using a straight-edged pastry wheel or sharp knife, cut the dough into 4cm squares or diamonds.

Return to the oven until dry and crisp but not brown, about 30 minutes. Transfer to a wire rack to cool. Serve warm or at room temperature.

Dante Milani

Master Knifemaker

'Could you make me a knife? *Oggi*... today?' I'm of the school of home cooks who would argue that a proper knife is a kitchen's most essential tool. But, like the schoolchild who assumes that milk comes from the supermarket, I've only ever thought of knives as coming from the shop. And so my question is equal parts query and request. I have no idea whether it's even remotely possible to make a knife in one sitting, but if it is, I'd like 82 year-old *mastrocoltellaio* Dante Milani to make me one.

He answers by reaching for a bundle wrapped in the pink pages of the *Gazzetta dello Sport*, laying it on the dusty steps of his workshop, and unpacking a collection of hand forged knives. '*Come lo vuole?*' His wide grin displays a full set of improbably straight, blindingly white teeth. I pick up a pocket knife by its carved wooden handle and unfold the shiny blade. '*Attenzione,*' Milani says, reminding me of the obvious: these knives mean business. He hands me an ash-grey, stag horn handled dagger – the sort favoured by wild boar hunters. Archaic, vaguely frightening and beautiful, I can't imagine ever finding a use for it. '*E questo?*' I ask, eying a leather-handled tool with a heavy, silver blade, shaped like a giant comma. '*Ah!* The famous *pennato di Monterotondo,*' he says, eyes sparkling under his blue baseball cap. 'Designed by my great grandfather Salvatore to lop branches and shoots off trees.'

I ask him whether he has something a bit more... ordinary. He retrieves a second bundle from a cardboard box, unwraps it and there they are: a row of cook's knives, so humble and plain I can understand why they aren't the first ones he brought out, though their simplicity is lovely. I pick up one after the other, settling on a knife which feels properly weighty but not unwieldy. It has a blade just shorter than the length of my outstretched hand and curved like the prow of a boat, and a smooth wooden handle the colour of wild honey. I like everything about it – except that I haven't seen it emerge out of metal and fire.

'Ach. That's the easiest knife to make,' he says dismissively, as if my request will hardly allow him to demonstrate the full breath of his skill. 'But if it's the one you want...' His voice trails off as he turns to light the forge, setting a match to a wad of crumpled newspaper nesting in a bed of black coals. Zara, the beagle, curls up in a corner, yawns and drifts off to sleep. She's seen this show a thousand times.

* * *

Milani picks up a metal rod and holds it to the flame until it glows as red as the coals. Then he lays it on the anvil and begins to hammer it flat with a steady, rhythmic pounding whose shrill ring hangs in the air long after the rough blade has been broken from the rod.

It seems that Milani abides by whatever health and safety standards were in force in the early 1900's when his father first opened the workshop in the hill town of Monterotondo Marittimo. The beamed ceiling is covered in thick, black soot – the forge has no chimney and the room is ventilated by the chance breeze that happens through the shop's open doors – but Milani appears none too worse for the wear. *Al contrario*. Hammer in hand, whistling as he refines the blade, he seems not only to possess the strength of a man half his age, but also to take a guileless, almost childlike delight in his work.

When the raw blade is cool, he rummages through a box of rectangular wooden blocks looking for a handle, holding bits of rough-hewn wood up to the blunt heel of the blade as if searching for the one shoe that will fit. '*Questo è bellino*,' he declares, clamping the chosen piece into a vice, sawing a slit down the centre, and pushing in the blade.

Next he starts up the grinder. Gloveless, he skates the blade back and forth across the spinning wheel, while sparks shoot out like fireworks. When the edge is razor sharp and silvery, he sands the wooden handle down to its finished shape; then, measuring by eye, drills three holes into the handle and tang (the bit of blade that extends into the handle), and holds his work up for inspection. 'This knife can do anything in the kitchen.'

So why is he slipping the blade out of its handle, rather than hammering in the rivets? For one simple reason: the knife is useless until the blade has been tempered. '*Quello che conta è tutto qui*,' Milani states emphatically. This is what counts. 'People think tempering is some sort of secret knowledge,' he says, stoking the fire. 'It just takes years of practice. *Guardi*!' He holds the blade to the flame and in minutes the metal turns from gold to violet to grey. 'You learn to judge exactly how long to heat the metal so that the blade will be strong but not brittle.' He drops it into a bucket of olive oil to cool, then sets a pot of water over the dying embers of the forge.

* * *

'You know you need to take care of this knife, don't you?' he asks, slipping the blade back into its handle and hammering in the rivets. 'It will rust if you don't dry it properly. And the wood will need oiling.' I don't mind. This is a knife I want to take care of.

He hands it to me ceremoniously then walks over to the forge and drops a handful of dry pasta, a chunk of meat, and half a sausage into the simmering water. I look at him quizzically. '*La pappa del cane*.' Zara's supper.

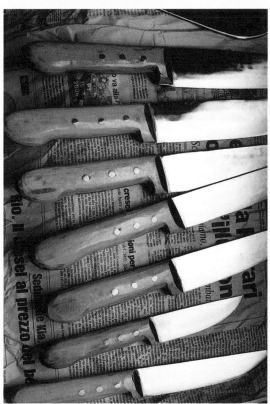
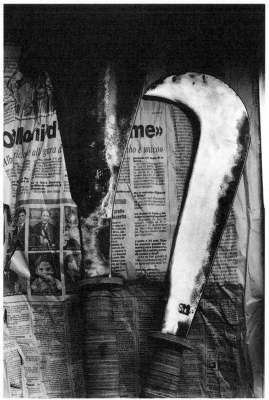

RIBOLLITA
TWICE-BOILED TUSCAN BREAD SOUP

SERVES 6–8

400g dried cannellini beans, soaked in cold water overnight

6 tablespoons olive oil, plus extra to drizzle

2 garlic cloves (unpeeled)

4–5 sage leaves

few black peppercorns

sea salt and freshly ground black pepper

2 onions, chopped

2 carrots, thickly sliced

2 celery stalks, thickly sliced

2 potatoes, peeled and cut into chunks

1 bunch of cavolo nero or kale, coarsely chopped

½ small Savoy cabbage, coarsely chopped

1 large bunch of Swiss chard, coarsely chopped

400g canned plum tomatoes, chopped

300g day-old (or older) coarse country bread, preferably unsalted

Drain the beans and put into a heavy-based cooking pot with 2 litres water, 2 tablespoons olive oil, the garlic, sage and peppercorns. Cover and cook over a low heat until the skins are tender and the beans are soft, about 2 hours. Season with salt three-quarters of the way through cooking.

Use a slotted spoon to scoop out about half of the beans; set aside. Pass the remaining beans through a mouli or purée in their cooking water, using a hand-held stick (or free-standing) blender.

Heat 4 tablespoons olive oil in a heavy-based cooking pot on a medium-low heat and cook the onions until soft and translucent. Add the carrots, celery, potatoes and leafy vegetables. Stir for a couple of minutes, then add the tomatoes. Cover and simmer over a low heat for 20 minutes.

Stir in the puréed beans and simmer, covered, until the vegetables are very soft, about 1 hour. Season to taste with salt and pepper.

Break the bread into pieces and add to the dense soup with the reserved whole beans. Simmer until the bread softens. Remove from the heat, allow to cool, then refrigerate overnight.

The next day, preheat the oven to 180°C/Gas 4. Ladle the ribollita into an earthenware casserole and bake, stirring occasionally, until it is heated through, about 45 minutes. Don't stir for the last 15 minutes to allow a light crust to form. Ladle into bowls, drizzle with olive oil and serve.

CINGHIALE IN DOLCE E FORTE
SWEET & SOUR WILD BOAR

SERVES 6

for the boar

1.5kg wild boar meat, cut into chunks

750ml red wine

200ml red wine vinegar

sea salt and freshly ground black pepper

6 tablespoons olive oil

1 yellow onion, finely chopped

1 carrot, finely chopped

1 celery stalk, finely chopped

2 bay leaves

1 tablespoon plain flour

500ml beef or chicken stock, plus extra as needed

for the sauce

2 tablespoons raisins

100g plain, dark chocolate, chopped

15g salted butter

1 tablespoon sugar

2 tablespoons pine nuts

2 tablespoons candied citron, chopped

2 cloves

pinch of freshly grated nutmeg

125ml red wine vinegar

A day in advance, rinse the meat well, then place in a bowl with 500ml red wine and the wine vinegar. Cover and leave to marinate in the fridge overnight.

The following day, drain the marinated meat and sprinkle with salt. Warm 1 tablespoon olive oil in a large frying pan, add the meat and sauté just long enough for it to release its liquid, about 5 minutes. Remove the meat from the pan with a slotted spoon and set aside. Discard the liquid.

Heat the remaining 5 tablespoons olive oil in the frying pan and add the onion, carrot, celery and bay leaves. Cook gently, stirring regularly, until the vegetables are soft but not browned. Return the meat to the pan, increase the heat and brown on all sides.

Season with pepper, then sprinkle with the flour and stir well until it is absorbed. Pour the remaining 250ml wine over the meat, reduce the heat to low and simmer until most of the liquid evaporates.

Bring the stock to a simmer and pour over the meat. Cook over a gentle heat, uncovered, until the meat is tender, about 2½ hours, adding additional stock if the pan dries out.

Prepare the sauce while the meat is cooking. Soak the raisins in warm water to cover for 10 minutes, then drain. Melt the chocolate and butter in a heatproof bowl over a pan of hot water. Stir in the sugar, raisins, pine nuts, citron, spices and wine vinegar. Remove from the heat and set aside until the meat is cooked.

Pour the sauce over the meat in the pan, increase the heat to medium and stir for several minutes to coat the boar in the sauce, adding a bit of stock to the pan if needed. Remove the cloves and serve.

PAPPARDELLE SULLA LEPRE
PAPPARDELLE WITH HARE SAUCE

SERVES 8

for the sauce

1 hare, about 1.5kg, with lungs, heart and liver
120ml white wine vinegar
5 tablespoons olive oil
1 red onion, finely chopped
1 carrot, finely chopped
1 celery stalk, finely chopped
1 rosemary sprig (leaves only), finely chopped
5 sage leaves, finely chopped
2 bay leaves
sea salt and freshly ground black pepper
120ml dry white wine
400g canned plum tomatoes
200g brine-cured black olives, pitted

for the pappardelle

800g '00' pasta flour
large pinch of salt
8 large eggs
4 tablespoons olive oil

to serve

freshly grated parmesan

Cut the hare into large pieces and rinse under cold running water (with the offal), then soak in cold water with the wine vinegar added for 1 hour. Rinse and pat dry.

Heat the olive oil in a large, heavy-based flameproof casserole over a low heat. Add the onion, carrot, celery and herbs, and cook, stirring occasionally, until the vegetables are soft but not browned, about

20 minutes. Add the hare, turn up the heat and brown on all sides. Season with salt and pepper.

Add the wine, lower the heat and let bubble until it evaporates. Add the tomatoes, olives and 200ml water. Cook on a low heat for 1 hour, stirring regularly. Set aside to cool.

When cool enough to handle, pull the meat off the bone, shred with your fingers and return to the pan.

To make the pasta, pile the flour into a mound on a clean surface (ideally marble). Make a well in the centre and sprinkle with the salt. Break in the eggs, add the olive oil and beat lightly with a fork. Use one hand to swirl the egg mixture in a circular motion, slowly drawing in the flour from the sides until a rough mass forms. Shape the dough into a ball and place on the remaining loose flour.

Wash your hands and clean the surface. Now use both hands to work in just enough of the remaining flour to make the dough tacky and not dry. Clean your surface once again and knead the dough until it is smooth and elastic, adding extra flour in small increments if the dough becomes too sticky.

If rolling the dough by hand, wrap it in cling film and let it rest for 20 minutes to 3 hours before rolling. Divide the dough into 2 or 3 pieces and dust your surface and rolling pin with flour. Lay a portion of dough on the surface and firmly but gently roll the dough out from the centre, rotating it regularly so that the dough flattens evenly. Turn the dough over occasionally and dust with flour to keep it from sticking. When the dough is thin but not transparent, use a straight-edged pastry wheel to cut 15mm wide strips.

To roll out the dough by machine, follow the manufacturer's instructions, starting with the rollers on their widest setting and gradually narrowing the setting as you feed the dough through repeatedly, until the rollers are on the second finest setting. Cut each length of dough into 15mm wide strips.

Boil the pappardelle in abundant salted water for 2–3 minutes. Drain, toss with the hare sauce and pile into warm bowls. Serve with grated parmesan.

Luciano Casini

Chef/Proprietor: Il Chiasso

My friend Peggy Markel who teaches cookery and leads gastronomic adventures in Tuscany, Sicily and Morocco tells a story about the first time she met Luciano Casini. She'd heard fantastic things about his restaurant il Chiasso and had arranged a meeting. 'When I asked for directions, he said, *"Pay-ghee… when you get to Capoliveri, walk up the steps towards the main square and call my name."* I sort of furrowed my brow but agreed. It was dusk when I trudged up the steps leading into the village. Nobody was around, so I called 'Luciano!' Quietly at first, then 'Luciano!' a bit louder. 'LUCIANO!!' The next thing I know, a bespectacled head pops out of a window, and a mischievous voice bellows out, *"O-o-o-h! Sono io Luciano!"*

Luciano Casini possesses the sort of larger-than-life personality that eclipses everything within its orbit: Too big to fit behind an office desk. Too irreverent for something like politics. Possibly too much to be married to. Perfect for acting (which he's done as a sideline). Better still for the benevolent ruler of a small kingdom, which is as good a description as any of the way he runs il Chiasso. The restaurant sits amidst the tangle of narrow alleyways off Capoliveri's main square on the island of Elba, its name a reference to the lane that cuts right through the middle of it.

* * *

Until I'd spent some time in Tuscany, I didn't realise it had its very own Mediterranean archipelago, made up of Elba (Italy's third largest island after Sicily and Sardinia), Giglio and the tiny islands of Giannutri, Montecristo, Capraia, Gorgona and Pianosa. Guidebooks would have visitors know that Elba is most famous for being the island of Napoleon's exile. Truth is he lived there for less than a year and his brief presence is exploited more as a tourist attraction than anything else. Mainland Tuscans adore Elba – despite the fact that it is overcrowded with sunburned holidaymakers all summer long. But what stretch of European coastline isn't?

The town of Capoliveri is sprawled on a hilltop overlooking some of the most splendid stretches of the island's coastline. In the old days (when people spent more time defending themselves against marauding invaders than working on their tans), the hill towns must have been the safest places to settle and build churches and watchtowers and airy *piazze* shaded by impressive, leafy trees. Capoliveri is one of those places.

Luciano opened il Chiasso 35 years ago, on his return from nearly a decade in Germany. I'd imagined he'd been drawn to the restaurant business for reasons as obvious as the love of good food and drink. He wasn't. 'I moved to Munich when I was 17 to look for work. I'd studied to be an electrician, but actually I had no intention of becoming one of those people who has to get up every morning at 7:00am to go to work. I've always been lazy in the morning. *Mi piace la notte. Amo le persone della notte.*' 'I like night,' he says. 'I love night people.' His eyes sparkle roguishly and I get the feeling he's about to tell me the real reason he's chosen the restaurant life. 'A Persian friend of mine found me a job as a waiter. I was fascinated by the customers. And you know what? When you're fascinated by them, they are fascinated by you. *È bellissimo.*'

There is a pause in the conversation, which Luciano fills with the statement, 'I love me so much.' Another pause. 'This is not egoism… not narcissism,' he adds, to correct any impression he might be giving to the contrary. 'You must love yourself in this life or you're lost, you're out of balance.' Luciano likes to hold forth… it's the actor in him.

'Money isn't life. Sure, it gives you the chance to live a bit better, but what counts is human contact. Laughing, having fun, touching life.' From anyone else this might be hyperbole, but Luciano walks his talk. You can see it in the way he and his crew sit down to an early meal like a family around the dinner table; you can see it in his relationship with his customers.

Actually, he doesn't much like the word customer. 'A 'customer' is a transient. Even if you only come here once, you're a guest. Maybe we'll become friends, maybe not. That's not the point.' He lights a Marlboro and reaches over to the table behind us (where some German friends of his are having dinner) and pours himself a glass of wine. Luciano thrives on reciprocal generosity: he is as likely to give you a bottle of wine as he is to nip a glass from a bottle you've paid for.

* * *

Despite the fact that love of all things gastronomic is not the driving motivation behind il Chiasso, the food is wonderful. Today we've eaten impossibly tiny *totanini* (squid) and bluefish dredged with flour and fried; home-cured *ventresca* (tuna belly) with white beans; spaghetti with garlic, tomato, wild fennel and *boga* (a local fish); and *fave con l'uovo*, a traditional stew of broad beans, artichokes and peas, which is not as beautiful as you might imagine (the veggies are cooked to a dullish grey and the whole thing is topped with a fried egg), but very tasty and nutritious.

Polpo (octopus) is a fixture on the restaurant's menu in one guise or another: *polpo con patate* (octopus stewed with potatoes, tomatoes and rosemary); *zuppa di polpo* (octopus soup); *carpaccio di polpo* (paper-thin chilled slices of braised octopus). '*Polpo* used to be the *cibo dei poveri* (poor man's food) on Elba,' Luciano explains. 'It was sold on the street by octopus fishermen – to be taken home and cooked, or eaten on the spot as an afternoon snack. The *polpaio* set up a table with a hole in the middle. Underneath sat a huge pot of boiled octopus. There were forks in a glass jar. You'd ask for a *granfia di polpo* and the *polpaio* would skewer an octopus from the pot, slice off a tentacle and hand it to you on a fork. There would always be a bar across the street. You'd eat your polpo with a glass of wine. If you couldn't afford a glass of wine, the *polpaio* would give you a glass of the water the octopus was cooked in.'

It is Saturday night and by this hour every table in the restaurant is filled; a few unlucky ones have been turned away. The kitchen is in a fury of activity; servers scurry around wielding plates heaped with gifts from the sea; the air is laden with the hum of a dozen conversations. 'I love food, you know,' Luciano says, surveying the scene. 'And if you eat at my table it's important to me that you eat well. But that in itself is not enough. There should be some connection, some exchange, some way in which we're both touched so that the time here becomes an experience we both remember and not simply a meal.'

FAVE, CARCIOFI, PISELLI E POMODORINI ALL' UOVO
BROAD BEANS, ARTICHOKES, PEAS & TOMATOES WITH EGG

SERVES 4–6

1kg broad beans in their pods

1kg peas in their pods

6 small artichokes, cleaned down to their edible hearts and leaves (see page 120)

juice of 1 lemon

4 tablespoons olive oil

1 white onion, finely chopped

12 cherry tomatoes, halved

sea salt and freshly ground black pepper

6 large eggs

Shell the broad beans and peas and set aside. Cut the artichokes into wedges and immerse in a bowl of cold water with the lemon juice added.

Warm the olive oil in a medium frying pan over a gentle heat. Add the onion and cook until it is soft and translucent.

Drain the artichokes and add to the pan with the tomatoes, broad beans and peas. Season with salt and pepper and cook, stirring occasionally, until the vegetables are soft. Add a little water if necessary to keep the pan from drying out.

Make 6 hollows in the vegetables and break an egg into each. Cover the pan and cook until the egg whites are opaque, but the yolks still soft. Serve at once.

TOTANI FRITTI
FRIED SQUID

SERVES 4

800g small to medium squid, cleaned

150g plain flour

sea salt and freshly ground black pepper

750ml sunflower or grapeseed oil to deep-fry

2 lemons, cut into wedges

Cut the squid body pouches into 2cm rings. Leave the tentacles whole. Season the flour with salt and pepper. Dredge the squid in the flour, shaking each piece lightly to remove any excess.

Heat the oil for deep-frying in a suitable heavy-based pan until hot but not smoking. To check that the temperature is right, drop in a piece of squid: it should sizzle immediately on contact with the oil.

Deep-fry the squid in batches until light golden in colour, about 3–4 minutes depending on size. Remove with a skimmer, drain and carefully blot between sheets of kitchen paper.

Sprinkle the squid with salt. Serve immediately, with lemon wedges.

POLPO CON LE PATATE
OCTOPUS WITH POTATOES

SERVES 4

1 kg octopus, cleaned
1 yellow onion, halved and very thinly sliced
2 ripe tomatoes, peeled, chopped and deseeded
1 rosemary sprig (leaves only), finely chopped
1 dried chilli, broken into pieces
generous splash of olive oil
1 kg potatoes, peeled and cut into chunks

Cut the octopus into bite-sized pieces and place in a heavy-based pan over a very low heat. Cover and let the octopus release its liquid, removing the pan from the heat after 10–12 minutes. Drain the octopus, reserving the liquid; set aside.

Put the onion, tomatoes, rosemary and chilli in a separate pan with a splash of olive oil. Cook over a gentle heat until the onion is soft and the tomato has reduced to make a thick sauce.

Add the octopus to the sauce. Cover and cook over a low heat for about 20 minutes, then add the potatoes. Cook until the potatoes are soft and the octopus is tender, about 30 minutes. If the pan seems to be drying out, add some of the reserved liquid from the octopus. There is no need to salt this dish.

SPAGHETTI AL CHIASSO
LUCIANO'S SPAGHETTI

SERVES 4

400g fresh saltwater fish of any type, filleted
sea salt and freshly ground black pepper
400g dried spaghetti
3 tablespoons olive oil
1 garlic clove, crushed
generous handful of cherry tomatoes, halved
few fennel sprigs, chopped

Cut the fish into small bite-sized pieces, discarding any skin; set aside.

Bring a large pot of water to the boil. Add salt, return to the boil, then add the spaghetti.

Meanwhile, heat the olive oil and garlic in a large saucepan over a medium heat. When the garlic is golden, add the fish and a grinding of pepper. Sauté for a couple of minutes, then stir in the tomatoes, fennel leaves and a ladleful of boiling water from the pasta pot.

When the pasta has cooked for 5 minutes, drain (reserving a ladleful of water) and add to the sauce. Toss well and cook the spaghetti in the sauce until it is al dente, adding a bit of the reserved water if the sauce seems too dry. Serve at once.

Famiglia Frullani

Chestnut Growers

'Most Tuscans only think of chestnuts as an autumn treat,' says Licia Frullani, as she scribbles out directions from her family's *agriturismo* to their *metato* (chestnut drying hut), a few miles down the road. 'Up here in the Apennine mountains, the chestnut tree used to be called *l'albero del pane*,' she explains. The bread tree. 'In hard times, it kept whole families alive.'

The wood was used for fuel and furniture. Chestnuts were eaten fresh – either boiled with bay leaves and fennel seed, or roasted over the coals of a chestnut wood fire. But by far the greater portion were brought to the *metato* for drying, then milling into what Licia calls *farina dolce*. Sweet flour. The flour was used for *castagnaccio* (a dense flat cake made a thousand different ways but always with chestnut flour, rosemary and nuts), *necci* (chestnut flour crêpes) and polenta. 'We poured the polenta on to a wooden board, cut it with a willow branch and ate it with a bit of ricotta.' It was sweet, but it wasn't pudding. 'It was everything.'

* * *

The chestnut season begins in October when the ripe fruits begin to fall from the trees. 'You can't rake them off their branches like olives,' Licia's husband Pietro explains. 'You have to wait until they drop off on their own.' In the days when a remote mountain community's survival depended on the abundance of the chestnut harvest, every able-bodied soul – grandparents and kids included – collected the nuts by hand. 'We walked around carrying hampers, or with big pocketed aprons tied around our waists. The harvest was so important – we couldn't let ourselves miss even one nut!' There's not a trace of wistfulness in his voice. Gathering chestnuts was backbreaking, dawn-till-dusk labour. Most of the *castagne* were hidden under fallen leaves, or had yet to free themselves from their finger-piercing, prickly husks. These days, the family hoovers up the harvest with an unwieldy contraption that collects the glossy brown nuts and spits out leaves and husks.

The Frullani's *metato* sits on the sloped edge of 2½ hectares of terraced chestnut woods. By late October the place has the feeling of an enchanted forest – trees bare; air grey and misty; the ground a carpet of dusky brown leaves and slippery grey stones covered with moss; the silence thick and woolly, broken only by a songbird's trill and the distant babble of water pouring over rock.

The drying hut is divided into two levels by a slatted floor – a slow fire smoulders on the bottom; the chestnuts are laid out to dry on top. For over half a century, Pietro's 94 year-old father Guiseppe tended the *metato's* fire. When the rigours of a 40-day job that began at dawn and ended around midnight became too great, his 77 year-old cousin Eligio offered to step in. This year's fire was lit on October 20th. Four times a day Eligio stokes it with chestnut wood, husks and last year's shells, then buries his efforts under shovelfuls of ash so the flames are tempered, but the heat maintained.

This morning's labour is to turn the chestnuts so that they dry evenly. Pietro and his son Leonardo grab two shovels and climb into the smoky *seccatoio* (drying room). They work at a companionable rhythm, the rasp of metal on wood and the patter of nuts tumbling off shovels their only conversation. Eligio watches from the edge of the *seccatoio*. He takes a knife from his pocket, cuts into one of the shells and pops a dried chestnut into his mouth. '*È come una caramella*,' he says, slicing open another nut so I can follow suit. It's as unyielding as a stone and about as flavourful. But my mouth is watering in a way that tells me it's understood it has been offered something edible. I persevere, and after about the time it takes to eat a bowl of pasta, the *castagno* finally relents and offers up its caramelly sweetness.

The *battitura* – threshing of the chestnuts – will take place in a fortnight if the weather's dry. Everyone is recruited for the dusty jobs of feeding the *castagne* through the ancient machine that removes their skins and shells, and sorting through the pale wrinkled nuts to toss out any that are burned or spoiled. The resulting cache will be carted up the hill to neighbour Daniele Petrucci's handmade wooden mill to grind into soft, sweet flour.

'There used to be *metati* scattered all over these mountains,' Eligio reminisces. 'Ours is one of the only ones still working.' A *corbello* (bushel basket) hangs off a nail under a covered porch next to the drying shed. The harvest is measured in *corbelli* – the Frullani's and those of neighbours who bring in their chestnuts to dry. This year 189 basketsful went into the *metato*. 'It's a lot of work,' says Pietro. 'We don't do it for the money. *Si fa per passione.*'

Pietro and Eligio 'tsk' disapprovingly when I ask them about large-scale commercial drying facilities, which have replaced the *metato* in some parts of Tuscany. 'If *castagne* are industrially dried,' says Eligio, 'they don't have *il sapore dovuto* (the right flavour).' And what is the right flavour? '*Dolce*,' they answer in unison. '*Con un tocco di amaro.*' Sweet… with a touch of bitterness.

ARROSTITE UBRIACHE
DRUNKEN ROASTED CHESTNUTS

Pierce the chestnut shells with the sharp tip of a knife. Roast the chestnuts in a perforated pan over medium-hot coals, turning them regularly in the pan so they cook evenly. When the shells are dark and brittle, and the chestnuts soft enough to put your teeth through (try one), turn them out into a shallow bowl. Douse liberally with red wine, cover with a tea towel and leave for 10 minutes. Return the nuts to the perforated pan, heat over the coals for a few minutes, then empty them out on to the tea towel. Shell and enjoy.

POLENTA DI CASTAGNE CON RICOTTA
CHESTNUT POLENTA WITH RICOTTA

SERVES 4

sea salt

400g chestnut flour

olive oil to oil

500g ewe's milk ricotta

Bring 1 litre water to a gentle boil in a heavy-based pan. Add a pinch of salt. When the water returns to the boil, pour in the chestnut flour in a fine, steady stream, stirring continuously with a wire whisk so that no lumps form.

After a few minutes when the mixture begins to thicken, lower the heat to a minimum and stir constantly with a wooden spoon until the polenta is the consistency of a stiff porridge, about 15 minutes.

Pour the polenta on to an oiled wooden board. Wait a few minutes until it sets, then cut into thick slices, with a piece of string held taut between your hands.

Place a few slices of polenta on each serving plate, along with a generous spoonful of ricotta.

CASTAGNACCIO
CHESTNUT FLOUR CAKE

SERVES 6–8

500g chestnut flour

sea salt

grated zest and juice of 1 orange

4 tablespoons olive oil, plus extra to oil and drizzle

3 rosemary sprigs (leaves only)

75g pine nuts

75g shelled walnuts, broken into pieces

Preheat the oven to 200°C/Gas 6. Oil a 23 x 33cm baking tin.

Put the chestnut flour into a mixing bowl and add a pinch of salt. Slowly pour in 650ml water, mixing constantly with a wooden spoon until you have a smooth, liquid batter. Stir in the orange zest and juice, then the olive oil.

Pour the cake mixture into the oiled tin and scatter the rosemary and nuts evenly over the surface. Drizzle generously with olive oil and bake for about 40 minutes until the crust is brown (dark, but not burned) and a fine skewer inserted into the centre comes out clean. Turn out on to a wire rack to cool.

Fabrizio Tiribilli

Potter

This is a story about generosity… and about a potter.

I first came across Fabrizio Tiribilli's work in a linen shop in Florence. I was hunting down props for a cookery book and had spent the day wandering in and out of shops that sold traditional majolica. This may sound like fun, but I was starting to have that glazed-eyed look one gets after a day at the Uffizi gallery. Too much beauty, too much to take in. And anyway, all I wanted was something that was beautiful and handmade, that wouldn't compete with the food I put on it. Lovely as they looked on display, I didn't want overripe pomegranates bursting all over the borders of a soup bowl, or dragons spitting fire on my *bistecca*.

So there in this little shop was a homely wooden table, laid with cloth napkins and these utterly plain, glazed terracotta plates and bowls. They were obviously handmade – not in an amateurish way, but because they had that slight variation from one to another which happens in things that aren't made by machine. And despite their total lack of adornment, they had depth and warmth. They were perfect.

'*È questi?*' I asked the shopkeeper. 'Ah. That's Fabrizio Tiribilli's work. Isn't it beautiful? He's a lovely man.' There was only one problem – she didn't stock his things because his output was limited and a lot of what he did was commissioned. 'Ring him up and see what he can do.' I scribbled down the phone number of his shop and studio, Radicchio Rosso, on the west coast of Tuscany in the town of Cecina.

Generally if you ring up a total stranger to ask if you can borrow some of their work, they are a tad sceptical. Usually they'll want some money, or at the very least a credit card deposit. Justifiably, they'll expect a credit in any publication featuring their work. But Fabrizio Tiribilli didn't want anything. He was so delighted that someone appreciated and understood what he was up to, that without our ever meeting, he arranged to have several boxes of goodies delivered, including a few things that weren't his design, which he thought I might like.

A few years later when I began working on this book, I remembered Fabrizio. I didn't know the details of his work and I didn't know a thing about his life, but my instincts told me it was a good one. I wanted to believe that if I followed generosity back to the source I would find a life well-lived. I did, and it is.

* * *

Radicchio Rosso has all the personality of the man who spends his days there. It is the first 'china shop' I've ever been to that has a sign on the door inviting the bulls to come in and play. He means it too. Fabrizio's childhood drawing desk is set up in a corner and filled with crayons, and there's a bucket of building blocks on the floor. Classical music drifts out of speakers somewhere; a table is set for an imaginary dinner party; there are stacks of dishes in 20 different colours on a shelf.

A voice called out from behind an arched doorway. 'Lori is that you?' It's always interesting to meet someone you feel like you already know but have never actually encountered face to face. It's like going to see the film of a book you've read – the characters never look exactly as you imagined them. Fabrizio had a striped linen apron tied around his waist and hands full of red clay. He held out an elbow for me to shake.

'Do you mind if I keep working while we talk?' The back room is his studio with rough brick walls and the assorted tools of his trade. He picked up a wooden pin and began rolling out a chunk of clay as if it were pizza dough. I glanced at the potter's wheel behind him. 'I throw bowls on the wheel, but a *piatto* (plate) I roll out and shape with a mould.' 'Did you always want to be a potter?' I asked. He laughed. 'No. When I was 20, I wanted to become a monk! Then I decided I'd be an artist. But when I really thought about it I realised that I wanted to make things that were useful.'

The fact is that when Fabrizio talks about his work he sounds like an artist – not pretentiously so, but because he speaks with the sensibility of someone whose ideas about his craft are strongly felt. He's the sort of person who begins a sentence with the phrase, '*se devo dire la verità*' (if I have to tell the truth), then tells you exactly

what he thinks, come what may. Somehow he manages to appear soft-spoken, while actually being exceedingly forthright. And so I learned why it is that his pottery is deliberately plain: 'A teacher of mine once said that we could do whatever we wanted so long as he could see our motivation for abandoning tradition. I agree. You have your roots and you evolve from there.'

To illustrate his point, he searched through his bookshelves, pulled down a thick volume and furiously thumbed through its pages until he found a photograph of the staircase to the Biblioteca Lorenziana in Florence designed by Michelangelo. 'Do you see how this was a total departure from tradition? The stairway is so massive and the entrance to the library so small. I think he did it to remind people that they were entering a place of learning.'

Fabrizio's own work has been influenced by Rothko's rich, shimmering use of colour. 'I love working with colours. There's so much depth in just one hue.' His studio is lined with jars of powders and pigments, each a story unto itself. Nothing is what it seems. A glaze that looks gunmetal grey when it is applied might turn peacock green after firing. 'I've developed all my own glazes through experimentation and trial and error. It's always still a mystery though. You may have done something a thousand times, but until you open the kiln, you don't know what you'll find.'

* * *

At 1:00pm he locked up the shop and we headed over to La Mariola farm for lunch. Fabrizio's wife Enrica is an agronomist. She left her job when they started a family – their girls Matilde and Vittoria are now 6 and 4. La Mariola is Enrica's labour of love – an organic apricot orchard and *agriturismo* with four cheerful apartments overlooking the village of Santa Luce, in the hills northeast of Cecina.

Santa Luce (Saint Light) has the authenticity of a place that is neither a destination in itself, nor on the way to one. There is laundry flapping in the breeze, lots of *nonni* with grandchildren in tow, one church, a post office, a general store and a bar that sometimes doubles as a trattoria. On market days the shops come to it – Tuesdays a few stalls sell fruits, vegetables, cheeses, cured meats and seedlings for the garden; Wednesdays are for knickers, clothing and cheap plastic toys.

We ate outside under a wooden pergola: summer vegetable soup ladled over toasted bread rubbed with garlic; baked round green courgettes stuffed with mince; and a dense apricot torte still warm from the oven. The girls ate everything the adults did, only more quickly. Matilde chattered all through lunch. Vittoria only seemed shy – she was first to jump up from the table and climb the lattice sides of the pergola, gleefully ignoring her parents' pleas to 'get-down-from-there-right-this-minute.'

After lunch we took a digestive amble through the countryside. The unpaved road that runs past La Mariola is lined with honeysuckle, rock roses, garlic, fennel, borage and buttercups – and those are just the wild things. Wheat fields and olive groves surround the *agriturismo* and its 1,500 apricot trees. The orchard looked wild and untamed, though its trees were full of fruit. 'I have a non-interventionist approach to growing,' Enrica explained. 'Apricot trees don't like to be pruned and they don't mind grass around their ankles. I'm not interested in forcing them to over-fruit, so there's really not much to do but leave the trees alone.'

We picked a handful of ripe apricots and ate them standing in the tall grass. More than any other fruit I know, a shop-bought apricot and a home-grown one are two entirely different creatures. Commercial apricots might trick you into thinking they're going to taste like something with their peachy skins demurely blushing pink, but half the time they're insipid and mealy. These apricots dripped juice down our chins and made our hands sticky – and they tasted like honeyed nectar, or like something the gods dreamed up when they were imagining the perfect end to a summer's day.

ZUPPA DI VERDURE ESTIVE
SUMMER VEGETABLE SOUP

SERVES 6

4 tablespoons olive oil, plus extra to drizzle

1 yellow onion, chopped

1 leek, chopped

1 carrot, chopped

1 celery stalk, chopped

4 small new potatoes, peeled and cut into chunks

handful of green beans, halved

2 courgettes, sliced

1 ripe tomato, quartered

sea salt and freshly ground black pepper

100g cooked cannellini or other white beans

250g Swiss chard, ribs and leaves coarsely chopped

¼ medium Savoy cabbage, roughly chopped

6 slices country bread

2 garlic cloves, peeled

Warm the olive oil in a large cooking pot over a medium heat. Add the onion, leek, carrot and celery and sauté gently for 5 minutes.

Pour in 1.5 litres water, stirring well. Add the potatoes, green beans, courgettes and tomato, and season with salt and pepper. Simmer, uncovered, for 20 minutes.

Add the white beans, chard and cabbage leaves, and simmer, partially covered, for a further 15 minutes. Check the seasoning.

Before serving, toast the bread and rub with the garlic. Lay a slice of bread in the bottom of each warm bowl and ladle the soup over. Drizzle with olive oil and serve.

ZUCCHINE RIPIENE
STUFFED COURGETTES

SERVES 4

8 medium globe-shaped courgettes
100g day-old country bread
250ml milk
4 tablespoons olive oil
1 yellow onion, finely chopped
1 carrot, finely chopped
1 celery stalk, finely chopped
handful of flat-leaf parsley, finely chopped
300g lean minced veal
sea salt and freshly ground black pepper
pinch of freshly grated nutmeg
2 large eggs, lightly beaten
4 tablespoons freshly grated parmesan
4 tablespoons breadcrumbs

Parboil the courgettes in a pan of boiling water for 3 minutes, then drain. When cool enough to handle, slice off the top quarter of each one, so the stem end becomes a lid. Use a teaspoon to gently scoop out the flesh from each courgette, leaving a shell about 2cm thick; take care to avoid breaking the skins. Finely chop half the flesh and set aside (use the rest for another dish).

Preheat the oven to 180°C/Gas 4. Break the bread into pieces, place in a bowl and pour on the milk. Leave to soak for 10 minutes.

Meanwhile, warm the olive oil in a saucepan. Add the onion, carrot, celery and parsley and cook until the vegetables are soft but not brown. Add the veal, season with salt, pepper and nutmeg and cook until it is lightly browned and any liquid is absorbed. Remove from the heat.

Squeeze the bread to remove excess liquid and place in a mixing bowl. Add the meat and chopped courgette flesh, mixing well. Pour in the beaten eggs, add the parmesan and stir to combine.

Spoon the mixture into the courgette shells, sprinkle with breadcrumbs and put their 'lids' on.

Stand the stuffed courgettes in a roasting pan and bake for 40 minutes. Serve hot or warm.

TORTA DI ALBICOCCHE
UPSIDE-DOWN APRICOT CAKE

SERVES 8

for the caramel

25g unsalted butter, plus extra to grease tin
100g caster sugar

for the cake

10 apricots
3 large eggs, separated
180g caster sugar
120ml olive oil
120ml natural yogurt
2 tablespoons apricot jam
180g plain flour
1 teaspoon baking powder
pinch of bicarbonate of soda
pinch of salt

Preheat the oven to 180°C/Gas 4. Butter a 25cm round cake tin.

To make the caramel, melt the butter and sugar in a heavy-based saucepan over a low heat. Continue cooking until the caramel turns a warm amber colour. Carefully pour into the cake tin, swirling the tin to spread the caramel evenly.

For the cake, quarter the apricots and remove the stones. Lay the apricots in the cake tin, skin side down, beginning in the centre and radiating outwards so they are evenly distributed.

In a bowl, beat the egg yolks and half the sugar together until pale and creamy. Whisk in the olive oil, pouring it into the bowl in a slow, steady stream. Gently stir in the yogurt and apricot jam.

Sift the flour, baking powder, bicarbonate of soda and salt together and fold into the cake mixture. In another bowl, whisk the egg whites until thick, then whisk in the remaining sugar until soft peaks form. Carefully fold into the cake mixture.

Pour the mixture into the tin over the apricots and bake for 45 minutes or until a fine skewer inserted in the centre of the cake comes out clean.

Leave in the tin for a few minutes, then run a knife around the edge of the cake and invert on to a wire rack to cool. Transfer to a cake plate to serve.

MARMELLATA DI ALBICOCCHE
APRICOT JAM

Wash and stone 1kg fresh apricots and place them in a pan with 600g sugar. Mash the apricots with a wooden spoon and let them sit in the pan with the sugar off the heat for 30 minutes. Place the pan over a low heat and bring to a simmer. Cook gently until the mixture is the consistency of a runny jam, about 10 minutes. Spoon into sterilised jars and seal. Keep in the fridge and use like a fresh jam. Makes about 1kg.

Pietro Staderini

Artisan Coffee Roaster

'*Le faccio un caffé?*' 70 year-old Pietro Staderini asks me by way of greeting, raising his voice to be heard over the whirr of roasting drums – heating and spinning 60 kilos of Arabica coffee beans until they turn from muddy green to the rich brown colour of monks' robes. 'Shall I make you a coffee?'

Staderini has been asking this question nearly all his life – first as a fresh-faced 20 year-old who'd landed a job in one of Florence's best known bars (in Italy a *caffé* is the stuff you drink and a bar the place you drink it), then as proprietor of the artisan *torrefazione* (coffee roasting house) Piansa and the bustling bar of the same name. There is no shortage of places to drink coffee in Florence, but Piansa makes the only *caffé* I'd drive out of my way for.

'*Questo non è un caffé, è un cioccolato.*' This isn't a coffee, it's a chocolate. Staderini launches into a description of his current favourite coffee bean: Nova Moca from the archipelago of São Tome in the gulf of Guinea. It's a rare heirloom bean whose low yield (400 kilos of coffee per hectare as opposed to the 6,000 kilo yield of modern hybrids) is, in Staderini's opinion, more than made up for by the singular elegance and complexity of its flavour.

Staderini is dressed in the impeccable style of Italian men of a certain age – tie-less, with a fine wool jumper over a starched shirt buttoned up to the neck. His eyes are bright behind his wire-rimmed glasses, but there is something vulnerable about his smile and he looks smaller and rather more fragile than I remember him. I stir a spoonful of sugar into the coffee and ask him how he is. He picks up a tangerine and begins to peel it painstakingly slowly, as if he could spend the entire day absorbed in this one task. 'How should I be? I've lost my wife.'

Anna was Staderini's companion in life and in work. 'We were always together. She knew everyone who came to Piansa, remembered everyone's name. She was a fantastic cook... she made things no one makes anymore: *spezzatino di polmone con alloro* (stewed calf's lung with bay leaves); *anatra in porchetta con finocchio selvatico* (roast duck with wild fennel seed).'

Staderini met his wife shortly after he moved to Florence in the 1950's. 'It was another world back then,' he reminisces. 'The bar I worked at was famous for its espresso. We sometimes served 5,000 coffees a day!' The post-war economy was

booming. A coffee cost 20 lire – the equivalent of a penny today – and the average person could finally afford the luxury of buying ground beans to take home.

Staderini takes my empty cup and invites me into the roasting room. The first thing I notice is that the smell of coffee roasting is not the deep, rich smell of coffee being ground or brewed. Somehow I'd imagined it would be. This smell is warm, green and smoky, but also a bit like bread ready to come out of the oven – not unpleasant, vaguely homey even, but not the sort of scent I'd ever associate with coffee. Of course, coffee beans are like olives: you really wouldn't want to eat one straight off the tree (or bush), and you marvel at the genius who first figured out what to do with them.

'How can you tell good raw beans from bad ones?' I ask. 'You need to feel them, weigh them in your hands. You want them to be heavy. If they're light, they're empty inside and won't be good. If they smell too grassy, they'll be bitter. We test beans that look promising with a little machine that roasts 100 grams at a time.'

Stacks of 60-kilo burlap bags fill one side of the roasting room. They are printed with their place of origin – Santo Domingo, Ethiopia, Brazil, Kilimanjaro, Columbia and Costa Rica among them. Jamaican Blue Mountain coffee arrives in wooden barrels, and beans from Venezuela in small wooden crates. I'd noticed that Staderini's office was lined with faded photographs of coffee plantations. 'Have you visited any of these places?' I ask. He shrugs his shoulders, closes his eyes and 'tsks' in a way that, when combined with an almost imperceptible shake of the head, is Tuscan for no. '*Io in aereo non ci vado.*' He's never been on a plane and he's not about to start now.

Staderini guides me to the roasting machine and back to the reason for my visit. 'You know, Italians aren't actually the world's biggest coffee consumers, but I'll bet they are the most demanding ones.' They certainly are the most exacting. The specificity with which a coffee is asked for at a bar is astonishing. A basic espresso is simply called a *caffè*, but that's only the beginning. Said *caffè* can be, among other things: *lungo* (long) or *ristretto* (short); *macchiato* ('stained' *caldo* or *freddo* with hot or cold milk); *corretto* ('corrected' with a splash of grappa or other spirit); *shakerato* ('shaken' with ice and sugar syrup); or, in one of its favourite incarnations, doused with hot, frothy milk and sometimes a dusting of cocoa for a cappuccino.

It is self-evident that however good the barman, a coffee can never be better than the ground, roasted beans it is made with. Unlike industrial roasters, which roast a huge volume of beans quickly over extreme heat, Torrefazione Piansa roasts batches no greater than 60 kilos. In theory the roasting time is between 18 and 20 minutes. In practice the coffee beans are ready in what Staderini refers to as '*l'attimo fuggente*' (the fleeting moment), when they are smoking but not burnt, their scent sweet but not oily, and their colour just the right shade of brown. Towards the end of the roast Staderini checks the beans every 20 seconds or so with a probe that slides into the roasting drum and pulls out a random sample. When the beans are deemed ready, the machine spits them on to a metal grate, where they are quickly cooled and picked over by hand. 'Burnt beans rise to the top. Unripe beans don't turn properly brown.' The roasted beans are stored in jute bags for 4 days before being packed. 'They need to breathe. You can hear them popping in the bag as they settle down.'

According to Staderini, the finest Italian coffee is made from a blend of 80% Arabica beans and 20% Robusta. Arabica costs more because it's trickier to grow and needs high altitudes to thrive, but it is unquestionably the more elegant of the two. Robusta seems to have been named for its flavour. 'It has a lot more caffeine and can be woody and acidic, but a really high quality robusta rounds the coffee out.' He pauses then adds, 'Acidity is bad for the stomach, but a little caffeine is good for the brain – it helps you think clearly.'

A proper cappuccino

'A proper cappuccino,' says Staderini, is two-thirds
milk and one-third coffee – and should fit nicely
in a 250ml cup. It is neither a bucket-sized brew,
nor should it be topped with a litre of boiling,
soapsudsy milk (though some foreign coffee
houses better left unnamed would have us think
so). And, at least in Italy, it is not an alternative to a
post-prandial *caffè*.

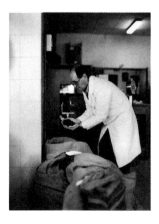

'The espresso should be made with 7 grams of
ground beans; the shot pulled for 15 to 16 seconds,
and in any event no longer than 20,' he explains.
The resulting coffee will have a light, hazelnut
coloured foam on top. The milk must be full fat, and
steamed so that it neither scalds nor separates into
hot liquid and dry froth. '*Deve fare una crema*,' he
insists, describing the particular creamy fluidity of
properly steamed milk. A dusting of cocoa powder
is permissible, though not essential.

ANATRA IN PORCHETTA
CON SEMI DI FINOCCHIO

ANNA'S ROAST DUCK WITH FENNEL SEEDS

SERVES 4

1 duck, about 2–2.5kg
3 garlic cloves, peeled
2 teaspoons salt
50g fatty prosciutto or lard, in one piece
2 tablespoons fennel seeds
freshly ground black pepper
olive oil for brushing

Preheat the oven to 200°C/Gas 6. Rinse the duck under cold running water and dry thoroughly.

Put the garlic and salt in a mortar and mash with the pestle to a thick paste. Finely chop the prosciutto or lard. Add to the mortar along with the fennel seeds, season generously with pepper and mash until the ingredients are well blended.

Massage the paste all over the duck and inside the cavity. Brush the skin lightly with olive oil and place the duck in a roasting pan. Roast in the oven for about 1½ hours, turning twice, until well browned and cooked through – the juices from the thigh should run clear when pricked with a fork.

Transfer the duck to a board or platter and rest in a warm place for 15 minutes before carving.

PANDIRAMERINO
ROSEMARY & RAISIN BUNS

MAKES 6

20g fresh yeast or 7g sachet easy-blend dried yeast

500g strong plain (bread) flour

2 tablespoons caster sugar

pinch of salt

90ml olive oil, plus extra for brushing

4 tablespoons rosemary leaves

200g raisins

In a small bowl, dissolve the yeast in 300ml warm water. Let the mixture stand for 10 minutes. The liquid will turn opaque and creamy.

Combine the flour, sugar and salt in a large bowl. Make a well in the centre and pour in the yeast liquid. With one hand, swirl the liquid, slowly incorporating the dry ingredients from the sides of the well until the mixture forms a rough dough. Wash your hands and lightly flour a work surface.

Knead the dough on the floured surface until it becomes smooth and elastic, about 7–10 minutes. Dust with additional flour if the dough is too sticky, or sprinkle with water if it feels too dry.

Clean your surface, dust it with flour, place the ball of dough on top and cover with a clean tea towel. Leave the dough to rise until it doubles in bulk, 1–1½ hours.

Meanwhile, warm the olive oil and 2 tablespoons rosemary leaves in a small saucepan over a low heat until the oil is fragrant, without letting the leaves turn brown. Leave the oil to cool, then strain, discarding the rosemary leaves.

Preheat the oven to 200°C/Gas 6. Once the dough has risen, push it down with your hands. Add the raisins, remaining rosemary leaves and infused oil, then knead the dough for a couple of minutes to incorporate the ingredients evenly.

Divide the dough into 6 pieces. Shape into round buns, place on a lightly floured baking tray and leave to prove for 30 minutes. Use a sharp knife to score the buns (with a hash sign). Brush lightly with olive oil and let them rest for 10 minutes, then bake for about 30 minutes until the buns are golden. Transfer to a wire rack to cool.

Contrada La Tartuca

Siena's Tartuca Contrada

To be perfectly honest, until recently I'd always considered Siena's Palio to be one of those hyped 'folkloric' events I'd happily go out of my way to avoid. We've all seen the pictures: the mad, bareback race around the Campo; the crush of flag-waving revellers lining the streets, perched on balconies, filling the square; the medieval pageantry; the sweltering summer heat. For heaven's sake, who would voluntarily subject themselves to such mayhem?

On the other hand, I've always been intrigued by Siena's *contrade* – the ancient division of the city into distinct boroughs – seventeen in all, each with its own church, heraldic flag, social house, fountain, museum and stable. It is the *contrada* which enters a horse in the Palio (through a series of complex machinations relying primarily on luck); the *contrada* church in which that horse is blessed by a priest on the day of the race; and the *contrada* which hosts its own Palio eve feast – attended by the jockey, the captain, various and sundry officialdom, supporters and anyone else willing to pay the reasonable sum required to secure a place at a table.

When I rang the Siena Tourist Bureau for information, I was put through to an officious sounding Signor Gigli who explained that no more than 10 horses run in a Palio, and that the *contrade* with horses entered in the race hold the biggest feasts. 'How many people attend?' I asked. He hesitated. *'Mille... mille cinquecento.'* 1,000–1,500. 'Who's in charge of the cooking?' 'The *contrada.'* 'I know, but who exactly?' I imagined him seated at his desk gathering patience. 'Everyone just helps.' I tried to comprehend the notion of volunteer cooks being responsible for a meal of this scale. This is Italy, and the gastronomic IQ is bound to be higher than in most parts of the world, but even so.

I battered him with questions. Which *contrada* has the best cooks? Who will have the most luscious feast? *Aquila... Bruco... Drago... Oca*? Eagle, silkworm, dragon, goose? I'd seen the various insignias fluttering on banners throughout the city, but at this point, the *contrade* were still much of a muchness in my mind.

'La Tartuca.' The turtle. *'Perché*?' I asked. *'Ci possiamo dare del tu*?' he answered with a question of his own. It never fails to feel like a significant breakthrough when an Italian asks if we can address each other in the familiar *tu* rather than the formal *lei*. It's an intangible sign of acceptance, of barriers tumbling, of a confidence about to be shared. *'La Tartuca* is my *contrada*. It's the only one I can speak for.'

The feast is meant to be propitious, Antonio Gigli explained. 'It's not so much about food,' he said, in the same breath telling me that he and his fellow *contradaioli* would be grilling 1,300 *bistecche* over open fires in the *contrada's* main square. 'We've won the Palio 50½ times, you know.' 'One half?' I asked. Laughter. 'In 1713, before the days of the photo finish, we tied.' And this year? 'Ah.' There was a smile in his voice. 'Luigi Bruschelli, nicknamed *Trecciolino*, is our rider. He's won more Palios than anyone. *Il cavallo* (the horse) is an unknown.' Ok then, I said to myself. Tartuca it is.

* * *

On the morning of the feast, Antonio met us at Porta Tufi, the southernmost gate to the city. It was the sort of day you hardly dare dream of in August – a midnight thunderstorm had blasted through summer's blanket of heat, leaving the air as sweet and light as autumn. The streets were still quiet, but it was obvious that we were in Tartuca territory. The sign of the turtle was everywhere: on blue and yellow flags flying from the *palazzi*; on silk scarves knotted around the necks of every living creature we passed; at the *contrada* fountain where a bronze turtle spouted an arc of water; tattooed on to the backs of wooden chairs in the square where the feast would be held.

We followed Antonio through the tree-lined *piazza*, past a row of tall iron braziers piled with kindling, into the Tartuca social house where the relative calm of the *contrada* dissolved into a flurry of activity. Every available surface was covered with trays of lasagne in various stages of preparation, and long rows of plastic white plates upon which the antipasto was being assembled. A handful of women wearing aprons over turtle t-shirts snaked through the room. The first arranged four slices of bresaola on each plate. A few steps behind her, another followed with a spoonful of *sott'aceti*

(pickled vegetables). A few black olives. A scattering of walnuts. It was the same story in the kitchen. Everyone had a task, yet no one seemed to be in charge. They were busy – not like bees in a hive, but like boisterous ants in a self-governed colony.

'*La rucola, ancora no*.' Too early for the rocket, announced a peroxide blonde who introduced herself as Aura. 'We don't want it to wilt.' I glanced at her friend Maria Irene who was spooning *sugo* from a huge pot on to a layer of pale yellow noodles. 'Don't be fooled by the industrial quantity. This is exactly the same recipe we cook for our families.'

The ladies clearly had better things to do than stand around chatting to an interloper about the workings of the *contrada*, but they granted me a few minutes anyway and introduced themselves by name and nickname. Antonella (Cascina) proudly told me she was born in Castelvecchio, the ancient heart of the *contrada*. Rosetta, who looked to be somewhere in her 60's, said she's volunteered to work at the Tartuca Palio feast since she was a girl. 'Imagine. I sleep in the same room I was born in. Isn't that amazing? For me, it's a great honour.'

It would seem that the *contrada* is an impenetrable society into which one must be born, or at the very least married. Not exactly. Angela, a journalist from Bari came to Siena for university in 1998. Three years later she was 'baptised' in the Tartuca's fountain. '*La contrada è una seconda famiglia*,' Angela explained. A second family. 'Here the collective reigns,' said someone else. 'The *contrada* is based on friendship… everyone is a volunteer… no one is in charge.' *La Tartuca* has made a habit of community. Its social house is open Tuesday nights for pizza, Friday nights for dinner. Proceeds flow back into the *contrada* coffers. It's impressive. Enviable.

* * *

We left them to a lunch of pasta with garlic, olive oil and chilli (served to the assembled volunteers out of a plastic washtub), and wandered over to the Campo – the great shell-shaped square where the race and all trials are held. Tourists milled about, looking slightly dazed, as if they weren't sure what they were supposed to be doing. There was an intensity about the locals, a feverishness in their gazes. It reminded me of soccer fans at a cup final. 'The Palio shouldn't be televised,' I heard someone say. 'You can't even begin to understand it until you've been to at least ten.' At two Palio's a year (one in July, another in August), that's a five-year apprenticeship.

Back at the Tartuca, the braziers had been lit and a crowd of *contradaioli* hovered at the cordoned edge of the stable, straining for a glimpse of their horse. Kids wore blue turtle t-shirts and Tartuca scarves; women, all manner of turtle regalia, from diamond broaches to tortoiseshell hair clasps. It was August 15th and the rest of Italy was at the seaside on summer holiday. Siena stayed home.

Clip, clop of hooves on cobblestone. 'Shhh.' The throng parted to make way for a fine-boned, wide-eyed, skittish brown horse named Elisir di Logudoro. The silence was absolute – until the moment the horse passed and the group fell in behind it, arm in arm, heads high, roaring chants as they marched through the narrow streets and into the Campo.

There was an undeniable aggressiveness in the air – and this was only the trial. The adolescents looked like soldiers going into battle, or ancient feudal rivals. One thing was clear: the Palio is anything but a tired spectacle held for the benefit of those of us who flock to Siena to bask in its pageantry. I felt a bit like a paparazzo. Or a gatecrasher at someone's wedding. Two hours later, 1,300 guests had taken their numbered seats at the long tables set up in the Tartuca's main square. There were speeches, chants, songs, revelry. The jockey shook hands with each of the Tartuca's 180 volunteers. Unbelievably, the steaks arrived at the table properly browned on the outside, juicy and pink inside, accompanied by a wedge of lemon, and a green salad dressed with olive oil and salt. There were envelopes at each table requesting a pledge of money if the Tartuca horse won – serious cash in the form of a discretionary sum to be paid in monthly instalments. Bribery money? Who knows? The rules to this game are ancient indeed.

* * *

The race itself – a mad, death defying, free-for-all – took all of 90 seconds. In the end, Elisir di Logudoro didn't win the Palio after all – *Contrada La Selva's* horse did. The winners ran through the streets to the cathedral to wait for the arrival the victor's silk Palio banner. Tartuca's *contradaioli* linked arms and headed home.

BISTECCA ALLA BRACE
GRILLED STEAK

SERVES 2

750g T-bone or porterhouse steak, cut from the rib with the bone

sea salt and freshly ground black pepper

2 tablespoons olive oil

1 lemon, cut into wedges

Take the meat out of the fridge 2–3 hours before grilling to bring it to room temperature. Prepare a medium-hot barbecue or grill.

Lay the steak on the barbecue or grill rack and cook, without turning, for 5–7 minutes, or until the exterior is brown and juicy. If the barbecue coals flame up, spray them lightly with water. Turn the meat over and sprinkle with salt. Grill for another 5–7 minutes.

Transfer the meat to a board, season with salt and pepper and drizzle with olive oil. Serve with lemon wedges.

RAPE SALTATE
SAUTEED BITTER GREENS

SERVES 4

2kg cime di rapa (or use sprouting broccoli)

sea salt

3 tablespoons olive oil

2 garlic cloves, crushed

Trim the cime di rapa or sprouting broccoli down to its florets and tender leaves. Add to a pan of lightly salted boiling water and cook for 5 minutes, then drain well. Roughly chop the greens when they are cool enough to handle.

Warm the olive oil and garlic in a large frying pan. When the garlic is golden, add the greens, season with salt and sauté briskly until the oil is absorbed and any liquid in the pan has evaporated.

LASAGNE AL FORNO
LASAGNE

SERVES 6–8

for the meat sauce

3 tablespoons olive oil
1 yellow onion, finely chopped
1 carrot, finely chopped
1 celery stalk, finely chopped
1 garlic clove, crushed
1kg lean beef, minced
250g lean pork, minced
2 bay leaves
sea salt and freshly ground black pepper
400g canned plum tomatoes, crushed

for the béchamel sauce

50g butter
40g plain flour
1 litre milk
generous pinch of salt
pinch of freshly grated nutmeg

for the pasta

500g packet dried lasagne sheets, or 1 recipe
fresh pasta dough made with 500g unbleached
flour, 5 eggs and sea salt (see page 164)

to assemble

butter to grease dish
250g parmesan, freshly grated

To make the meat sauce, warm the olive oil in a
large heavy-based saucepan. Add the onion,
carrot, celery and garlic and cook over a medium
heat until soft, stirring often. Add the minced meat
to the pan, breaking it up with a wooden spoon.
Add the bay leaves, salt and a generous grinding
of pepper. Increase the heat to high and stir well
until the meat is evenly browned. Stir in 250ml
water. When the liquid comes to the boil, lower the
heat and simmer, partially covered, for 45 minutes,
stirring from time to time.

Add the tomatoes and simmer over a low heat until
the sauce has thickened, about 45 minutes.
Discard the bay leaves.

To make the béchamel sauce, melt the butter in a
saucepan over a low heat. Add the flour and stir
continuously for 2–3 minutes until thickened, but
not brown. Heat the milk in a separate pan to just
below the boil. Slowly pour the hot milk on to the

roux mixture, whisking constantly until smooth. Add
salt and nutmeg and cook, stirring, over a low heat
for about 3–4 minutes until the sauce is creamy
and thick enough to flow from a spoon. Take off the
heat and set aside until cool.

If using homemade pasta, roll the dough out by
hand or by machine (following the directions on
page 165) and cut into 12 sheets, 30cm long,
7.5cm wide.

Cook the lasagne sheets in a large pot of boiling
salted water. Handmade sheets take 1 minute only;
dried lasagne need to be cooked until they are
firmly al dente. Immediately drain the pasta sheets,
rinse under cold water and dry on clean tea towels.

Preheat the oven to 180°C/Gas 4. To assemble
the lasagne, butter a 23 x 30cm baking dish. Set
aside a generous ladleful of meat sauce.

Cover the base of the dish with a thin layer of
béchamel. Arrange a layer of lasagne sheets over
the sauce, spoon one third of the remaining meat
sauce on top, cover with one third of the remaining
béchamel and dust generously with parmesan.
Repeat the layering sequence (pasta, meat sauce,
béchamel, parmesan) twice.

Add a final layer of pasta, cover with the reserved
meat sauce and sprinkle with parmesan. Bake in
the centre of the oven until lightly browned and
bubbling, about 30 minutes. Rest the lasagne for
10 minutes before cutting into portions to serve.

PANNA COTTA CON
FRUTTI DI BOSCO
PANNA COTTA WITH BERRY SAUCE

SERVES 6

for the panna cotta
2 teaspoons powdered gelatine
500ml double cream
150ml milk
100g caster sugar
1 teaspoon vanilla extract

for the berry sauce
500g mixed berries (strawberries, raspberries etc), hulled
75g caster sugar

For the panna cotta, put 2 tablespoons cold water in a small bowl, sprinkle in the gelatine and let stand for 10 minutes to soften.

Combine the cream, milk, sugar and vanilla in a heavy-based saucepan. Stir over a medium-low heat until the sugar dissolves; don't let it boil. Take off the heat and immediately whisk in the gelatine, making sure it is fully dissolved.

Pour the cream mixture into 6 ramekins or custard cups. Cover and chill overnight.

To make the sauce, put the berries in a saucepan with the sugar and crush gently with a wooden spoon. Let stand for 10 minutes, then stir in 60ml water. Cook gently until the sugar has dissolved and the berries are soft. Let cool before serving.

To serve, dip the base of each mould in hot water for about 20 seconds, then run a knife around the edge of the panna cotta and turn out on to a plate. Spoon over the berry sauce and serve.

LISTA DELLE RICETTE

LIST OF RECIPES

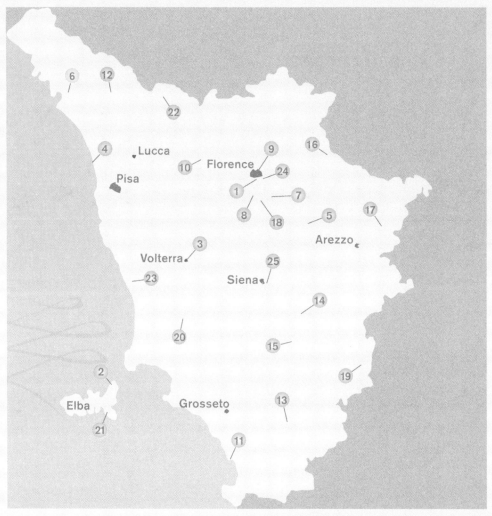

Location of producers

Contact information

**Trattoria Coco Lezzone
(Gianluca Paoli)**
Via del Parioncino, 26/r
50123 Firenze (FI)
+39 055 287178

**Azienda Agricola Ballini
(Roberto Ballini)**
Via della Parata - Loc. Monte
Grosso
57030 Cavo - Elba (LI)
+39 0565 949836
www.ballini.com

**Fattoria Lischeto
(Salvatore & Giovanni Cannas)**
Loc. San Giusto
56048 Volterra (PI)
+39 0588 30403
www.agrilischeto.com

Peperoncino (Massimo Biagi)
Via Parigi, 8
56124 Pisa (PI)

Paterna (Marco Noferi)
Cooperativa Agricola Valdarnese
Località Paterna, 96
52028 Terranuova Bracciolini
(AR)
+39 055 977052
www.paterna.it

**Larderia Colonnata di Fausto
Guadagni**
Via Comunale, 4
54030 Colonnata (MS)
+39 0585 768069

**Azienda Agricola Pruneti
(Gionni Pruneti)**
Via Case Sparse 22
50020 San Polo in Chianti (FI)
+39 055 855319
www.pruneti.it

Tripperia Pollini (Sergio Pollini)
Via dei Macci
50122 Firenze (FI)

**Tenuta di Capezzana
(Conti Contini Bonacossi)**
Via Capezzana, 100
59015 Carmignano (PO)
+39 055 8706005
www.capezzana.it

Pescaturismo (Paolo Fanciulli)
Porto di Talamone
58010 Talamone (GR)
+39 333 2846199
www.ansedoniaonline.it

**Osteria Vecchio Mulino
(Andrea Bertucci)**
Via Vittorio Emanuele 12
55032 Castelnuovo Garfagnana
(LU)
+39 0583 62192
www.ilvecchiomulino.com

**Aia della Colonna
(Famiglia Tistarelli)**
Località USI
58050 Santa Caterina (GR)
+39 0564 986110
www.aiacolonna.it

**Mario Mariani Artigiano
Terrecotte**
Via di Cappello, 29
50023 Impruneta (FI)
+39 055 2011950

Coltivatori di Carciofi di Chiusure
Associazione Castello di Chiusure
53020 Chiusure (SI)
+39 0577 707071

**Azienda Agricola Campi di
Fonterenza (Margherita &
Francesca Padovani)**
Località Fonterenza
99 Sant'Angelo in Colle
53020 Montalcino (SI)
+39 0577 844248
www.fonterenza.com

**Busatti (Famiglia Busatti
Sassolini)**
Via Mazzini, 14
52031 Anghiari (AR)
+39 0575 788013
www.busatti.com

**Pastificio Artigiano Fabbri
(Giovanni Fabbri)**
Piazza Emilio Landi, 17
50027 Strada in Chianti (FI)
+39 055 858013
www.pastafabbri.it

**La Frateria di Padre Eligio
(Walter Tripodi)**
Convento di San Francesco
53040 Cetona (SI)
+39 0578 238261
www.lafrateria.it

Dante Milani
Via Matteotti, 48
58025 Monterotondo Marittimo
(GR)
http://digilander.libero.it/milani
dante

Il Chiasso (Luciano Casini)
Vicolo N. Sauro, 9
57031 Capoliveri - Elba (LI)
+39 0565 968709

**Fattoria La Piastra
(Famiglia Frullani)**
Via Provinciale Torri di Popiglio -
Loc. Casetta
51024 Cutigliano (PT)
+39 0573 68443

**Radicchio Rosso
(Fabrizio Tiribilli)**
Via O. Marrucci 58a
57023 Cecina (LI)
+39 0586 635671
www.radicchiorosso.com

**Torrefazione Piansa
(Pietro Staderini)**
Via Meucci, 1
50015 Bagno a Ripoli (FI)
+39 055 645774
www.caffepiansa.com

Contrada La Tartuca
Via Pendola, 28
53100 Siena (SI)
www.tartuca.it

GRAZIE

Beaneaters & Bread Soup has been blessed with many helping hands along the way. From the moment we walked into Quadrille with our first enthusiastic musings, our publishing director Jane O'Shea understood the essence of what we were trying to do. Thank you Jane for believing that there was room in this world for another book about Tuscany, and for making our collaboration such a happy one. Heartfelt thanks to Janet Illsley, our editor in the trenches, for scrupulously ensuring that we always meant what we said, and said it properly. Our friend Lawrence Morton brought together images, prose and recipes and crafted a beautiful home for these portraits, so that each could shine individually and as part of the larger whole.

Cara, *dolce* Lisa Bartolomei, your friendship is a continual source of delight – *grazie* for the willingness with which you set aside your own important work to pick up ours and check the Italian for errors, gaffes and blunders. We are grateful to our friend and master-baker Claire 'Cakes' Ptak, for helping make sure this book's *dolci* would turn out as deliciously at home as they did in Tuscany – and for cheerfully searching out berries in the dead of winter. Stefano Landi, *grande amico*, saved the day with his camera when he stepped in for Jason on a warm summer night in Impruneta to photograph Mario Mariani firing terracotta pots and making *peposo* for his friends. A very big thank you to Laura Hynd who manages to keep in order Jason's chaotic professional life; and to Khadija Atif who helps keep our house a home at Podere Sala.

Some of the people featured in these portraits we have known and admired for many years. Others we discovered through what can only be described as a year-long Tuscan treasure hunt. The good work of the Tuscan agency ARSIA (Association for Development and Innovation in Agriculture) led us to

Monterotondo Marittima and the extraordinary knives of Dante Milani. Serendipity and Ryanair crossed Heather Jarman's path with ours. *Grazie* Heather, for your hospitality and for sharing your Garfagnana life with us. There's a whole book there – you should write it. Carla Capalbo's excellent book, the Food Lover's Companion to Tuscany has been a valuable resource for nearly 10 years. Many thanks to Slow Food fiduciaries Paolo Saturnini, Alessandro Draghi and Roberto Tonini for introducing us to some of their favourite people. *Mille grazie* to Hugh Cook, the most generous and talented gardener we know, for leading us to Massimo Biagi and his astonishing collection of chillies.

Several times throughout this project we reminded ourselves to make a record of all the people who so generously offered their help. Bits of that list can be found on countless scraps of paper, tucked inside the tattered pages of several notebooks, and scribbled upon the edges of maps that never made it home. To the guardian angels whose names have been left off these pages because of our own inefficiency and disorganisation – our sincere apologies and thanks.

Our family and friends are our greatest treasures. A deep bow to Ross, our brother-in-law, whose patience and generosity of spirit knows no bounds; and to everyone who took care of our kids, fed our bodies and souls, and picked up the slack when it all got too crazed. To our children Julien, Michela and Rae, for the enthusiasm with which they consumed vast quantities of wild boar stew, pappardelle with hare sauce, and whatever else was on the menu on any given recipe-testing day; and for understanding how much it meant to us to work together on a project we cared so deeply about. This book is also for you.

To all of you who allowed us into your workshops, fields, kitchens and homes so that your work could live within these pages: thank you for sharing your stories and your wisdom. We honour your work and the spirit with which you live your lives. Thank you for caring for the land, upholding traditions, pushing boundaries, remaining true to yourselves and your own personal visions of what makes a life well-lived, and finally, for reminding us that there are still so many good people in this troubled world.

First published in 2007 by
Quadrille Publishing Limited
Alhambra House
27–31 Charing Cross Road
London WC2H 0LS
www.quadrille.co.uk

Text © 2007 Lori de Mori
Photography © 2007 Jason Lowe
Design and layout © 2007 Quadrille Publishing Limited

Cataloguing in Publication Data: a catalogue record for
this book is available from the British Library.

ISBN: 978 1 84400 462 1

Printed in China

Publishing director Jane O'Shea
Creative director Helen Lewis
Project editor Janet Illsley
Designer Lawrence Morton
Photographer Jason Lowe
Extra photographs Stefano Landi
   (p4, 68, 72, 73 bottom left)
Production Ruth Deary